MW00452436

A Love Affair
with the Game

by Frank "Sandy" Tatum, Jr.

Foreword
by Tom Watson

Edited by
Martin Davis

FIRST EDITION

ISBN 1-888531-10-x

Published by:
The American Golfer, Inc.
200 Railroad Avenue
Greenwich, Connecticut 06830
(203) 862-9720
FAX (203) 862-9724

Design by:
ALL CAPS
599 Riverside Avenue
Westport, Connecticut 06880
(203) 221-1609

ACKNOWLEDGMENTS

We would like to thank Geof Russell, Brad Klein and Bruce Smith for their editing and fact-checking help. Thanks also to our art director and typographer extraordinaire Carol Petro for her invaluable assistance.

Dedicated to Warren Berl
whose love was and is
an inspiration for mine.

Table of Contents

GOLF COURSE ARCHITECTURE

MORE RUMINATIONS AND REMINISCENCES

EPILOGUE

Foreword

I met Sandy Tatum for the first time on the first tee of the Stanford Golf Club in the spring of 1968. I was an eager, longhaired and mustached member of Stanford's freshman golf team. He was an eager, silver-haired competitor for the Stanford Alumni. The event was the annual Stanford Golf Team match, the outcome of which was never in doubt. They drilled us!

During that particularly unforgettable day, I observed Sandy swing the golf club in a way I had never seen before. He started the swing just as any good golfer will, slow and with good position. But then something at the top of the swing appeared to go wrong—or, in his case, right. Instead of stopping the back swing by turning his hips towards the target, his whole motion simply stopped as if someone had pushed a "pause" button. Then, after more than a second, he started his downswing, just as if the "pause" button had been released.

This odd element of his swing is Sandy's trademark, but it's much more than a memorable quirk. I believe it is the reason he has retained his length well into his early eighties.

In the more than thirty years since we met, Sandy has been both a great friend and mentor to me. Knowing him as I do, I can honestly admit I have never met a golfer who has been so thoroughly possessed with the game. He has given immensely to the game in ways which cannot be fully measured in terms of his playing ability or his leadership in the sport, including the presidency of the USGA. The passion with which he lives golf is one immeasurable factor.

That passion attracted me to him in the early years of my professional career. Over the years, I have been privileged to share many days both on and off the golf course with Sandy and his family, and those are times for which I will be forever grateful. Two of our many experiences are worthy of mention here.

The first occurred on the fifth green at the Robert Trent Jones Sr.-designed Spyglass Hill Golf Course during our bi-annual partnership in the Bing Crosby Pro-Am. The weather, always the main topic of conversation during The Crosby, of course performed as expected. A hailstorm halted play and, while we waited for the ice to melt, Sandy read a humorous excerpt from a book his caddie—and son, Chris—was carrying for him, John Steinbeck's *The Log from the Sea Cortez*. The excerpt described the Hansen Sea Cow; a small outboard engine that only worked when the weather was perfect and the wind was at your back.

Here we were, weather-delayed, cold and wet, and Sandy was reading Steinbeck, highlighting the irony of it all. You might say it was there on the fifth green of Spyglass that I first realized the depth of his addiction (love) for golf.

The second experience I want to mention was during my first Irish/Scottish links golf trip organized by Sandy in 1981 before the British Open. He introduced me to Ballybunion and Royal Dornoch, as well as Old Prestwick, Kummel, and Royal Troon. I was the defending Open champion so our play drew more than a few spectators, especially at Ballybunion and Royal Dornoch. This caused only one minor problem for me, and it simply was that so many people following us (there were no gallery ropes) made it difficult to really see the surroundings of the course. So, after our first round at Royal Dornoch, one of my favorite links courses in the world, I quietly pulled Sandy aside from the after-round festivities and said we needed to play another round so that I could see this gem in all its splendor. Without hesitation, Sandy organized the caddies and off we went, unnoticed.

It was during that round of golf in a driving rain that I mentioned to Sandy, and truly meant it, that I had never enjoyed playing a round of golf so much. And I can still say it. Just he and I, the two caddies, and a £10 Nassau, which he luckily won. It was then and there my own love affair with links golf was consummated.

Sandy's love for the game is reflected by what he has given back to it. He continues to work for the USGA, designs and oversees the building of golf courses, and is a father who takes his sons on long golfing journeys. He has competed in numerous international events well into his seventies and has proven that, even with the yips, he can be a winner.

Ah, that terrible word, yips. For the non-golfers who may be reading this, the "yips" are uncontrollable flinches that can occur when one is attempting to putt, chip, or, in instances, drive the ball from the tee. Yips have caused countless retirements from the game as well as increased putter sales by the millions.

Sandy has a bad case of the yips. But the truly defining championship characteristic about Sandy is his unflappable statement that he will never, ever, give in to the yips and that someday he will overcome his terrible affliction and be off to greater heights.

That is pure passion for the game.

That's Sandy.

Thank you, Sandy, for sharing that passion with me so many years ago.

—Tom Watson

The Genesis
and Development
of a
Love Affair

Genesis

Golf has a host of distinguishing features. Among the more important are the legions of lovers of the game whose lives have been profoundly affected by the love affair. I had the good fortune to be a son of a father, Frank Sr., who was a consummate lover of the game of golf.

He and my mother had four children, of whom I was the youngest. Inexplicably, my father failed in his effort to transmit to my three older siblings an understanding of why he so loved the game and, therefore, why each of them should as well.

It may only have been the law of averages working in my favor, or perhaps he had learned from those failures to be a more effective transmitter. In any event, his successful approach to the process of recruiting me was unusual.

Having waited impatiently until I reached the age of six, he introduced me to the object of his love by occasionally taking me with him on Sunday to a sparsely played course where his Sunday game had been arranged. When we arrived at the course, he equipped me with two sawed-off hickory shafted clubs (the advent of steel shafts was still some years in the future) and three balls. He simply told me to stay out of the players' way while I played with that equipment and, when I got tired, to go sit in the car. It was some hours later when I saw him again after his game and post-game festivities, during which I had been in and out of the car several times. Looking back it is hard for me to believe, but the fact is I thought that was a perfectly wonderful way to spend a Sunday!

Having hooked me, he played me with a virtuosity that ensured that I, too, was hooked for life. His technique had the virtue of simplicity. He made playing golf or otherwise experiencing the game (e.g., as a caddie or spectator) a reward for exemplary behavior and performance. As he increasingly set the hook, he steadily raised the standards that would yield the reward. The benefits for me from that process were substantial. It secured my love of the game and provided a constant stimulus to develop as effectively as I could somehow manage.

As soon as I developed the strength and stamina to carry his very heavy golf bag (there was no limit to the number of clubs a player could use in those days) the reward element was extended to being invited to caddie for him. I have since wondered whether he could possibly have known how much I relished those reward occasions when I could, in a sense, share and most effectively observe a consummation of his love affair. The rewards, moreover, extended to getting fifty cents a round, which was doubled to a dollar when I got lucky and could add the bag of a fellow player. My good fortune extended to having a group of friends at or near my age who were almost as hooked as I was. We all understood that we were privileged to be able to play the game and we respected the opportunities accordingly.

The ultimate playing reward for me was to be invited to play with my father. On rare occasions my behavior achieved a level that justified adding to that reward a game with a friend and his father.

An incident that occurred on one of those "ultimate reward" days provides insight into how my father managed my development. On the fifth hole I missed a shot with my hickory shafted spade mashie and reacted by throwing the club. (While I understand that it is immaterial, I nonetheless note that the club only traveled a short distance and was observed only by my father.) As I approached the green, I felt his presence walking alongside me. He quietly said "You will not say anything to anyone. You will simply pick up your ball, return to the clubhouse area, sit behind the 18th green and remain there until you have further word from me."

Of course I did as I was told. The three of them played out the round and went into the clubhouse. After the sun had gone down and I had been sitting in the dark for some time, the locker-room steward came out and informed me that my father said I could now go sit in the car. Some time later he got in the car and started driving home. About halfway there, intently focused on the road, he said, "I have just one question: Will you ever again in any circumstance ever throw a golf club?"—to which I replied "No sir, I will never again in any circumstance ever throw a golf club." The subject thereby was permanently closed, and, while the provocations on many occasions have been grossly severe, there is no possible way that I could let go of the club.

Having been so initiated into the cult of lovers, I have spent an exhilarating portion of the rest of my life in fervent pursuit of the Grail that is a consistently effective golf swing. That lifelong adventure has stimulated some thoughts, exposed me to some personalities and involved me in some experiences which I am moved to share with whomever may be interested.

How I Became 'Sandy'

I am one of those people who has a nickname that bears no relationship to my given name. It is a name, moreover, which virtually all my friends and acquaintances use. To the extent that I have any public identification it is the name with which I am most frequently identified.

The name was attached to me in the following circumstances. I was the fourth child in my family and, before I was born (I hasten to add), my mother and father had decided that I was to be the last. Since they had two boys and one girl they were confidently anticipating that I would be a girl who would be named "Kathleen."

When my oldest brother was born, my mother had beseeched my father to name him Frank Jr. My father would not agree. The same process occurred on the birth of my older brother. When I appeared as a male, my mother, without consulting my father, had me identified on my birth certificate as Frank Jr.

My father's reaction to this development was alleviated by a telegram that I received at the hospital on the day of my birth. It came from a close friend of my father, a Scot named Scotty Chisholm who was a golf reporter, photographer and commentator on the then-*Los Angeles Examiner*. Scotty's Scottish heritage was emphasized by his wearing kilts at local golf events. His telegram to me congratulating me on my choice of parents was addressed to "Sandy MacNiblick Tatum." My father seized on that development to promulgate the use of "Sandy."

Scotty also honored the occasion with a droll bit of poetry dedicated to me:

"Who's the stranger, mother dear?
Look he knows us—ain't he queer?
Hush my own, don't talk so wild,
He's your father dearest child."
He's my father no such thing!
Father died away last spring.
Father didn't die you dub!
Father joined a golfing club.
But they've closed the club, so he
Has no place to be you see.
No place left for him to roam
That is why he's coming home.
Kiss him—he won't bite you child;
All them golfing guys look wild."

My father expressed his opposition to having a Frank Jr. on the premise that he did not want anyone opening his mail. I rather think he questioned whether any of his children could be a worthy successor to that name. As I came to know him I could understand that concern.

Wilshire Country Club, Howard Hughes, Katherine Hepburn and Bobby Jones

The Wilshire Country Club in Los Angeles has a special golf course. When the course was built, it was located some distance west of the developed area of the city of Los Angeles. As the city grew, however, the course came to be surrounded by residential neighborhoods and bifurcated by Beverly Boulevard, a major artery, so that the first nine is located south of the boulevard and connected to the second nine and the clubhouse location by a tunnel.

As I was growing up in Los Angeles in the 1920s and 1930s, I enjoyed the privilege of playing golf at Wilshire. Playing there included a routine that I followed whenever it was remotely possible to do so. I would take my clubs with me as I bicycled to school and stash the clubs in some bushes near the school so that at the end of the school day I could bicycle the considerable distance to Wilshire and play golf until it was too dark to be able to see the ball. I always played with two balls—one designated as being played by Bobby Jones and the other designated as being played by Walter Hagen. The competition that I so arranged between those two giants of the game was always very intense and very competitive. Somehow, however, Jones always managed to win and always on the final green.

Some of those golf games exposed me to a relationship, that, in the early 1930s, even in Hollywood, would have been identified as at least a bit of a scandal. It turns out that Katherine Hepburn was living with Howard Hughes.

My exposure to that relationship came about with a combination of unusual circumstances. Hughes then had a home directly behind the ninth tee, with a gate from his garden opening onto that tee. Hughes was a member of the club and a very good golfer, although most of his golf was reclusively arranged. Katherine Hepburn was a respectable golfer in those days. She was living there with Hughes. Hughes frequently would call the pro shop located on the north side of Beverly Boulevard to inquire whether anyone was playing on the first nine. When he was assured that it was all clear, he would order a caddie to meet him and Katherine on the ninth tee. What the pro shop did not know, however, was that I was often out there on that nine intensely engaged in yet another titanic match between Jones and Hagen. I was, therefore, a witness on several occasions to the stunning visage of Katherine Hepburn attired in slacks, which were not often seen on women in those days, and a loose-fitting sweatshirt with sleeves pushed up above the elbows and with that sensational head of auburn hair piled on the top of that beautiful face engaged with compelling intensity in a game with Howard Hughes. Even the stimulus of a Jones/Hagen match could not match the stimulation induced in a 13-year-old boy by that scene!

It was at that course where I had the privilege of being among a dozen or so people who watched Bobby Jones play a round of golf. The scene for that experience started in a classroom in the junior high school where I was doing a bit of daydreaming which led me to look out the window where I saw what I first thought was an apparition, but which turned out to be my father wildly waving his arms and signaling that I should join him. My first reaction was the dreadful thought that there had been a death in the family, but reflection provided the comforting conclusion that if that were the case, he simply would have gone to the principal and taken me out of class. I was left with no explanation for his somewhat bizarre behavior but to wait impatiently for the end of the hour when I could make contact with him. When I finally did so, he said, "Come on, Bobby Jones is playing golf at Wilshire!"

After a rather wild ride, we arrived on time to see Jones drive from the first tee. He was paired with Charlie Seaver (a semi-finalist in the 1930 Amateur at Merion and Tom Seaver's father), who was an outstanding amateur golfer. Jones and Seaver were playing an informal match against the Dutra brothers. Olin Dutra won the 1934 U.S. Open; his brother, Mortie, also was a very good professional golfer.

I do not recall who won the match. I do recall vividly the thrill that I experienced from watching Bobby Jones play a round of golf. We can all use heroes, particularly those who live up to our perceptions of them. Twelve year old boys have a special need for heroes. I was fortunate to have Bobby Jones as one of mine and he more than fulfilled all of my perceptions of him.

With exposure to the likes of Bobby Jones and Katherine Hepburn in their respective primes, a young boy had reason to understand that pursuit of the Grail that is the game of golf was going to expose him to some interesting people. Using his wildest imagination, however, he could not anticipate how many of them in fact there were going to be and how much they would enrich his life.

Stanford

Playing golf on the Stanford University golf team was a wonderful experience. The Stanford golf course then was stunningly beautiful and sensationally challenging. My teammates, individually and collectively, were a delightful lot. We were most fortunate to have a coach, Eddie Twiggs, who cared profoundly about the game, with emphasis on respect for tradition and for the rules and for playing the game in the proper spirit of sportsmanship. He was a fascinating personality and an excellent teacher.

Stanford golf teams in the later 1930s and early 1940s were national powers, which added considerably to the experience of being a part of them. College golf in those days, moreover, was kept in proper balance with the rest of the university experience. The golf season was confined to the spring, we played dual matches against other then Pac 8 teams and we only left the region to play in the NCAA championship. The matches were played at match play. The NCAA individual championship was also at match play. Stroke play, which determined the NCAA team championship, was confined to the 36-hole qualifying for the match play. All that added up to a combination of factors that perfectly fit my perceptions and feelings about golf and my convictions about how playing it should integrate into the opportunity of having four years of Stanford education and experiences.

Stanford was located in what then was a pristinely beautiful bay-created valley blessed with a glorious climate. The "then" in that sentence relates to the fact that someone today speeding down one of the crowded freeways scarring the landscape cluttered with buildings cannot imagine that the area once was covered with fruit trees which, when they blossomed in the spring, made it a harbinger of the Garden of Eden.

Idyllic is the closest I can come to classifying the Stanford experience for me embellished by playing on the Stanford golf team.

The golf part of that experience had a triumphant climax possibly qualifying as a saga. In my senior year the team had dominated the Pac 8 and we were relishing the anticipation of defending the NCAA championship the team had won the previous year. It was an awful blow, therefore, to be told that the athletic department did not have the funds to send us to South Bend, Indiana, where Notre Dame was hosting the championship.

I could not bear that blow without at least trying to find a way to raise the money. I was told that doing so would require the approval of the president of the university. Ray Lyman Wilbur was a formidable person who had been the Secretary of the Interior in the Hoover cabinet. He presented a gaunt and austere presence augmented by dark suits and high, stiff shirt collars. It was with considerable trepidation and very little confidence that I approached his office that had no foyer and was identified by a simple door with a glass panel containing the word "President." My knock elicited a muted invitation to enter. The office was long and narrow with one window at the far end. Dr. Wilbur was seated at a large ancient roll top desk with his gaunt upper body profiled by the light from the window. Dr. Wilbur was writing and continued to do so without looking at me when he said "What is it that you want to see me about, young man?" He continued writing as I told him. When I finished, Dr. Wilbur stopped writing, reached into a cubbyhole in the desk, pulled out a checkbook, wrote a check for twenty-five dollars and for the first time turned and looked at me as he handed it to me saying, "Good luck, young man." He then returned to his writing.

I managed to raise the money. We went to Indiana and successfully defended our NCAA championship. The ultimate crowning glory to the saga is that I won the individual championship.

Reflecting on that experience leads to some thoughts about what has since happened to the college golf scene. It has become woefully out of balance with the rest of the experiences young men and women should be having in their college years. Like so much of the other college athletics, it has assumed an importance grievously out of proportion to the other elements of a college education.

NCAA Division I-A golf has become consumptive of time critically important to the development of college students. Much too much time at the campus, and especially away from the campus, is taken with the playing of a game. For virtually everyone privileged to have the opportunities of a college education, those years should provide time to develop maturity in growing from an adolescent to a young person, to expand intellectual capacity and, above all, to get, at the very least, a sensible education. (I especially like the definition of an educated person provided by Wally Sterling when he was President of Stanford University, to wit: "An educated person is someone who can entertain himself/herself, entertain a friend and entertain an idea.") The time and energy Division I-A golf now requires of the players make it virtually impossible to achieve the personal development that the whole college experience can provide.

There is a related problem in this scene. Young men and women are attracted to competitive golf on the premise that it will lead to a career as a touring professional. They, therefore, are willing to sacrifice a complete college education to the achievement of that relatively narrow goal. For virtually all of them the goal turns out to be an illusion, because the numbers of them who in fact achieve it are statistically insignificant. The consequences for too many of them are distressing and frequently devastating. They have lost the opportunity for a real college education and their initial adult experience is to suffer a career failure.

There has been some movement recently to rectify this imbalance in the college experience; it needs to move a whole lot farther.

The Oxford Experience

I had the privilege of being a student at Oxford University at a time (1947-49) which I think may have been the best of all possible times. World War II had been won. We had survived that terrible war, which certainly was terrible however necessary it was to fight it and however salutary was the victory. There were no limits on the possibilities for our lives, which we then thought were going to be lived in a manageable world dedicated to peaceful and just solutions to problems and conflicts.

In that environment, the aura of Oxford University took on considerable added dimensions. Furthermore, in my first meeting with my law tutor he asked, "What game do you play, Tatum?" When I told him it was golf he said, "Right! We certainly cannot let this law study interfere with that!"

My golf career at Oxford started with a note pinned to the Balliol College bulletin board stating that anyone desiring to play on the Oxford University golf team should take out a card (as it put it) and record the score of a round played on a specific date at the strangely appealing golf course located in the city of Oxford. I did so and returned my card to the professional recording a 75.

Some days later, I was in my room studying when an undergraduate appeared at my door, introduced himself as the Secretary of the Oxford University golf team and stated that he was there to extend on behalf of the Captain of the team an invitation to me to be a member of the team. While I was delighted to accept, I could not have known how wonderful the ensuing experience would be.

We had no department of athletics and no coaches. Everything was handled by undergraduates who were members of the team. The Captain made the decisions on foursomes pairings (i.e., alternate shots played by a pair with a single ball) and team lineup.

We played somewhere every Saturday and every Sunday, except for the Christmas vacation, from early October until the middle of March. So many golfers also played cricket that the seasons for the two sports could not be allowed to overlap.

In the two years I played on the team there was never a game canceled on account of the weather, or otherwise. We played in conditions that included gale-driven sheets of water and courses frozen solid with wind-aided chill factors well below freezing. That experience gave me an attitude that has had lifelong utility. I am simply not concerned about what the weather conditions may be when I set off for a round of golf.

In the culminating event of the year we played Cambridge. All the other matches were against club teams at the considerable number of clubs with good courses that are located in and around London.

We would leave Oxford by bus early Saturday morning. When we arrived at the club, we were introduced to the team we were to play over coffee in the lounge. Typically, the weather would be perfectly awful. Also typically there was present an old gentleman who at the appropriate moment would stand reflectively looking out of the picture window at the awful weather and say, "Oh, I say, I think it is lifting!" That was the signal for us to suit up and play in weather that surely could have caused calling off the invasion of Normandy.

The day's play consisted of foursomes in the morning and singles in the afternoon. The noon lunch was embellished with a considerable quantity of alcohol, typically consisting of scotch or gin drunk before lunch, a good claret at lunch, followed by a vintage port with the cheese and a kummel with the coffee. Among the salutary effects of that alcohol consumption was the insulation it provided against the weather in which the afternoon round usually was played. The post game festivities were no less bacchanalian. I should note that the level of play was extraordinarily good and the competition suitably spirited.

While I had arrived at Oxford with an understanding of the benefits of alcohol moderately consumed, my appreciation for it was enhanced by such experiences. That appreciation lead to a remarkable experience.

On the Saturday night of those weekends we were housed in members' houses. On one Saturday, after the afternoon round, the Captain, with abject apologies, explained that I was going to be put at the home of a member who not only did not drink, but would not allow alcohol on the premises and that, since the old boy was an awful bore, I would have to suffer a very long dry evening. He further explained that there was no choice since the old boy had an American connection and had requested that I, as one of the very few Americans who had ever played for Oxford, be his guest.

The fact was that the old boy had a considerable capacity and regard for alcohol and had been told that the Oxford team posed a real housing problem, because it had this American on it who was a member of one of those abstruse cults that identified alcohol as the devil's product so that they had to find a place to put me up where there would be none of it consumed.

I cannot imagine how they persuaded the old boy to take me in. In order to be sure that the consequences were effectively memorialized, they sent along a brigadier general to be the observer and reporter.

When the three of us assembled, attired in our dinner clothes, I soon had come to realize how understated was the prediction of how long an evening it was going to be. The old boy was positively hostile and responded to my efforts to make conversation with monosyllabic grunts. After an interminable interval, the butler appeared carrying a silver salver on which was placed three crystal glasses and large bottle of orange squash, an unpalatable soft drink that somehow some people managed to drink in the U.K. The butler carefully poured each of us a glass. As the old boy attempted to swallow the stuff, he suddenly exploded at me saying, "You, sir, are the rudest person it has ever been my displeasure to have in my home!" When I sought some explanation for how I might have so offended him, he replied, "It is one thing to have some ridiculous concept about not drinking alcohol, but it is quite another to come into a person's home and insist that your host and his guests also abide by that ridiculous concept!" When I then explained what I had been told and that we apparently had been set up for the amusement of our respective friends, we figuratively fell into each other's arms and joyously (he turned out to be a perfect delight) embarked on a bacchanalian evening! So bacchanalian was it that the brigadier general observer went face down in his soup at dinner, causing the butler to remove his inert form and secure him in bed! So much for his report. My host and I carried on our celebration into the small hours.

The match with Cambridge was both the conclusion and the climax of the year. It was played at one of England's classic links. In my two years, Royal St. George's and Royal Liverpool (Hoylake) were the venues. The experience lasted a week, starting with matches with club teams and otherwise preparing for the climactic two days at week's end when the match was played. In those days it was an important event on the British amateur golf calendar. It was covered extensively by all the print media, including for *The Times* by Bernard Darwin, who may have been the best reporter of the game who ever lived.

The match consisted of foursomes and singles each over 36 holes played for a single point. At Royal St. George's my partner and I prevailed in the foursomes as did I in the singles. At Hoylake my partner and I earned a stirring victory in the foursomes, but a stymie on the 35th green undid me in the singles. Nevertheless, Oxford won again.

Hoylake, moreover, was the focus of a honeymoon of sorts for Barbara Snyder Tatum and me. Barbara, whom I had courted before going to Oxford, had accepted my proposal of marriage crafted in a letter dispatched from Ireland during the previous summer. We were married the day after she disembarked from the Queen Mary and, after three days in the Cotswolds, my bride found herself billeted with the Oxford team in an ancient small hotel located across the road from the 17th green at Hoylake. The weather that week varied between very cold and frigid, conditions that were exacerbated by consistent heavy winds. One of the features of the hotel was that the wind went through it with little diminution of velocity.

That experience had the utility of preparing Barbara for the first abode of our married life. The only place I could find in postwar Oxford was a room in an old rectory six miles outside of town that was an abandoned kitchen with a concrete floor and a single cold water spigot. It was furnished with a double bed, a rickety couch, a desk, a chair, and a two-place electric hot plate. We shared a bathroom with five other couples. Surviving those accommodations made the ensuing 50 years and counting of our marriage all downhill.

The Oxford equivalent of the "letter" awarded college athletics in the United States is a "blue." You win one by playing in the Match against Cambridge. Cambridge also awards a "blue" to its players who play in the match. The two blues are distinguishable by Oxford's being dark and Cambridge's being light.

Winners of blues automatically become members of The Oxford and Cambridge Golfing Society, a group that engages in a variety of golf activities. For example, during a summer vacation, I was a member of a Society team touring Scotland playing matches against teams provided at places such as Troon, Prestwick, Muirfield and St. Andrews. The matches, one in the morning and another in the afternoon, were played as foursomes.

The first venue of that tour was at Troon. My foursomes partner in the morning was Cyril Tolley, who was the premier British amateur golfer in the 1920s and 1930s. His match with Bobby Jones at St. Andrews in the 1930 British Amateur Championship stands as one of the classic matches of all time. Jones won it by laying Tolley a stymie on the 19th hole and went on to win his only British Amateur championship as a piece of his "Grand Slam."

That afternoon my foursomes partner was Roger Wethered. Roger's distinctions transcended being Joyce Wethered's brother. Joyce may have been the best woman player ever. Bobby Jones felt that way after playing an exhibition match with her at East Lake. Roger was a preeminent player in his own right. He could have won the British Open in 1921 had he not stepped on his ball while lining up a shot. The resulting penalty prevented his being in a playoff for the title. Anyone who has enjoyed the satisfaction of being a hero worshipper can appreciate what it meant to me actually to play with those two, especially as their respective partner.

The Society holds its annual golf championship at Rye on the southeast coast of England in the first week in January when the members gather to play for "The President's Putter." It is almost a certainty that the weather in that part of England in January will be awful. In view of general weather conditions in the United Kingdom, if golfers there were not willing to play in awful weather the game would never have developed there. It is a hardy lot of them who compete annually for "The Putter." They do so, moreover, playing two rounds a day in winter restricted daylight. If the U.S. PGA Tour with its legion of agonizingly slow players were to hold an event on that course in January, they would be hard pushed to get in one round!

The British have a philosophical phrase of wide application which is to "press on regardless." It certainly applies to playing in "The Putter," because you have no choice but to press on regardless of the weather.

One example of my experiences playing in "The Putter" illustrates that philosophy. It was seriously cold and it had been raining enough so that several cups were under several inches of water. There was no thought of suspending, much less canceling, play. Putting to those inundated holes required calculation of how hard to hit the ball so that it would come to rest in the water above the hole and then sink into it!

That philosophical approach dramatically contrasts with that of the PGA Tour manifested by the cancellation of the 1996 AT&T Pebble Beach National Pro-Am on the Monterey Peninsula because part of one of the fairways on one of the three courses used in that event, Spyglass Hill, had a casual water problem such that some of the players on that course might have to play a shot from casual water.

That AT&T Tour incident shows how far the game in this country, especially on the PGA Tour, has drifted from its origins in pursuit of "fairness." I rather favor the philosophy that you take the course as you find it and play the ball, if you can, from wherever you hit it. I like the approach of our Scot forebears who created the "rut iron" designed for playing shots from wagon wheel ruts.

There is a school of thought expressed in equipment advertisements that the best interests of the game would be served by making it easier. I disagree. It is the challenges which provide the siren call to attempt to deal with them. Making the game easy would reduce that call to a whisper.

The Swedish and Danish Amateur Championships

A further illustration of using the potential of the Oxford years is the trip that was arranged in the summer of 1948 to play in the Swedish and Danish Amateur Championships.

Three of us had the good fortune to share that experience. One of my fellow travelers was a Scot who had flown with the Royal Air Force in World War II, who was a delight to be with and whose enthusiasm for life engaged golf with a gusto that was a joy to behold. The other was an Englishman, Ted Harker, who also was a Royal Air Force pilot in World War II. He was my foursomes partner on the Oxford University golf team. Since he became such an important friend, I need to divert briefly to identify him further.

He was a lithe 6' 7" tall with an awesome arc in his golf swing that developed speed-of-light clubhead speed. The ball, therefore, was propelled prodigious distances, but not always, I have to say, in the intended direction. That characteristic made playing as his foursomes partner especially exciting. With the obligation to play the next one from wherever he hit it, I watched him drive with a mixture of excited anticipation and serious trepidation. I was either to be playing from some splendidly advantageous place or I was going to be confronted with a challenge that would have inhibited Arnold Palmer in his prime.

An insight into his flair and personality is provided by an incident which occurred when the two of us were playing a course for the first time. We came to a very long five-par on which Ted hit a prodigious drive down the middle. As he contemplated his second shot, he said to the caddie, "What do I need to get there?" The caddie responded, "Sir, I have been caddying here for 30 years. I have not only never seen anyone close to this green in two, I have never heard of anyone hitting it!" Ted then said, "Right! I will have my 3 wood, please."

There ensued a swing the dimensions of which defy description. The result, however, is readily describable. The only part of the clubhead which made contact with the ball was a small part of the heel so that the ball was propelled squarely between Ted's feet. Without a moment's hesitation, Ted handed the club to the caddie and said, "Right! I will now have my 4 wood, please." Whereupon he struck the ball so that it came to rest in the middle of the green! I like to think how often, and with such flourish, that caddie has recalled that incident in his local pub.

In addition to that, perhaps all that needs to be said about how much I revered my friendship with him is that when Barbara accepted my proposal and came to Oxford so that we could be married there, Ted Harker was my best man.

As Ted and I and the Scot, in the year before Barbara and I were married, flew to Scandinavia, we had to deal with a currency problem. UK citizens were then confined to £100 upon leaving the country. I, therefore, had to be the trio's banker. We were not exactly rolling in it, but, as will be developed, we managed spectacularly.

Our first stop was Bastad in Sweden to play in the Swedish Amateur Championship. There were very few golf courses in Sweden in 1948. The course at Bastad, however, was entertaining and challenging. They held the Women's Championship on the same course at the same time. The respective fields were small enough so that both could be accommodated at a dinner held on the eve of the championship. I was seated next to a young woman player who struck me on first impression as being extraordinarily attractive. As the evening started with a ceremonial downing of a shot of Aquavit washed down with some beer followed immediately by another like ceremony, that young woman became an eclectic of Ingrid Bergman and Marilyn Monroe! There was, moreover, an esprit to that dinner party that gave ultimate dimensions to that evening.

I was beaten in the semifinal. I struggle with the memory of how long I took to line up a 10-foot putt which I missed on the last green that I needed to take the match to extra holes.

With that salutary experience to bolster our respective enthusiasms, we sailed to Denmark. That championship was played on another engaging golf course located on the Danish Riviera north of Copenhagen. On the eve of that championship, a so-called Calcutta pool was held enabling enthusiasts to wager on the outcome. Since I was the only American in the field, I went for an awful lot of money to a middle-aged woman who, as I observed it, had to be a reckless gambler.

I progressed to the quarterfinals where I met a Brit who could play. We had a spirited match in which I played well enough to be dormie with two holes to play. I managed to foul up those two holes, so the match went to extra holes. My English and Scot travelling companions were remarkably interested spectators over those last two holes and around the first tee for the shot at the first extra hole. That hole was a short three-par with a very small green. My opponent struck a beautiful shot which finished six feet from the hole. I pulled my shot to the left of the green, leaving me an awkward, steeply downhill lie with a shot to play over a bunker with very little green with which to work.

As I left the tee, contemplating that predicament, I noticed my two friends, in a state of abject dejection, apparently heading for the bar. I took some comfort from the thought that they apparently cared so deeply about the outcome of my match.

There then ensued what then seemed—and still seems—to qualify as a miracle. I hit the impossible shot perfectly. It landed just over the bunker and rolled squarely into the hole! The shock effect on my opponent was such that his putt came nowhere near the hole.

In a euphoric state, I sought out my two friends in the bar. As I observed the disconsolate state in which they were consuming gin, I was struck yet again with how much it mattered to have friends who cared about me so deeply. When I told them what had happened on the extra hole, they required witnesses before they could believe it. It then developed that their apparent caring for me was in fact panic over the fact that they had bet every bit of our combined money that I would win. But for that miracle, we might yet be working our way out of Denmark. As it developed we were, relatively speaking, wildly rich.

My semifinal match went to the 36th green when I finally prevailed. As I walked off the green, I saw for the first time since her reckless wager the woman who had bought me in the Calcutta. She introduced herself, identified her interest in me and said, "I have a considerable stake in you and I am aware of the fact that the Englishman and Scot with whom you are travelling are not good for you to be with in the evening. Tonight I am going to see to it that you behave yourself. My car will pick you up at 6 p.m. and you will come to my house for the evening."

The car, which was a Rolls Royce, was there at the appointed hour, driven by a liveried chauffeur. Ensconced regally in the back seat, I was driven down the Danish Riviera until the car turned into a long winding drive ending at a lovely mansion. As I was escorted from the car, the front door of the house opened. My hostess was standing in it. As I approached her, I could see and hear a party in progress in the house which, to put it mildly, was spirited. As she took my arm to introduce me into the festivities, a butler appeared with a drink in a bucket-sized glass. My hostess then deposited me on a couch alongside what can best be described as a Norwegian female vision. As I settled into that scene, I had two related thoughts, to wit, "Here goes the Danish Amateur Championship, and it obviously will be worth it!"

A further thought then surfaced, which was to wonder what in the name of bacchanalian frivolity did she think I and my friends had been experiencing during the preceding evenings.

Soon thereafter, I got a glimmer of hope that the championship might not be a lost cause after all when I observed that the guest list included my opponent, who was engaging in the festivities no less enthusiastically than I.

In retrospect, I have concluded that my hostess had the sense that my opponent could probably beat me fair and square, but that I could deal with such an evening with more resilience. She was absolutely right. I won handily the next day and, therefore, have prominently displayed on my resumé "1948 Danish Amateur Champion!"

Muirfield, Henry Cotton and the King of England

As I contemplated my incredible good fortune to be gifted with two years at Oxford University, it was obvious that those two years offered opportunities that were not going to recur and, therefore, should not be missed. I managed to experience virtually everything I conceivably could. The range was remarkable; it included, as examples, a private audience at the Vatican with Pope Pius XII, and greeting then Princess Elizabeth and Prince Phillip at a small private party when they returned from their honeymoon.

It also included attempting to qualify for the British Open played at Muirfield in 1948. I played rather well in gale force winds to record a 75 in the first qualifying round and still had a chance as I teed it up on the 11th hole in the second round. I hit that shot, played into a stiff wind, as solidly as I could. When it failed to reach the fairway, leaving me in knee-high rough, I had to face the reality that qualifying for the British Open seemed, as Ben Hogan put it about holding the 12th green one year at The Masters, to call for a bit more skill than I had at the moment.

That failure, however, led to a unique experience. I was a witness to Henry Cotton playing a round in that Open with the King of England in his gallery for all 18 holes. When I arrived at the first tee before Cotton, I noticed a familiar figure standing in the gallery equipped with a shepherd's crook. I was suitably amazed when I realized it was King George VI.

Cotton, who broke through the barriers that had separated professional golfer from the members of private clubs, had developed an impressively regal persona of his own. I was not surprised, therefore, to see him appear in a liveried Rolls Royce from which he emerged near the first tee. As Cotton was introduced to the king before he teed off, it was abundantly clear who was more impressed with meeting whom. The king appeared to be restraining himself from asking for Cotton's autograph.

Cotton did, however, respond to the occasion with a majestic round of golf. Muirfield was playing fiery fast and the wind was blowing hard. As the king and I, together with several thousand others, watched in wonder, Cotton managed the course and conditions with a sensational 66. That set the stage for him to go on to win that Open decisively.

The king witnessed every one of those 66 shots. While there must have been some plain-clothed security in the gallery, there were only two uniformed bobbies. No one approached him or otherwise interfered with his concentration on the performance to which he was an enthusiastic witness. The behavior of that gallery toward him was a wonderful illustration of restraint and respect, which sadly are long gone from the current scene.

There were other memorable experiences too numerous to include in this chronicle. In sum, those two years at Oxford were indeed beyond belief wonderful and while I managed to earn a Bachelor of Civil Law degree, my life also was enriched with a putative Ph.D. in golf.

Some Extraordinary People

Luis Alvarez
and The Black Box

Among the extraordinarily interesting people with whom golf put me in contact was Luis Alvarez. Luis was a genuine genius and a physicist who was a Nobel Laureate, having received the Nobel Prize for expanding the frontiers of physics. He was a delightfully engaging person. Identifying him as "mad" is only justifiable because he was a certifiable golf nut, and when he was engaged in excited creativity his appearance often was a prototype of the mad scientist.

He was a member of a golf club that had no practice facility, so Luis created a device which enabled him to warm up at home for a round of golf. The device consisted of a platform on which to stand and make a full swing, during which the clubhead at the bottom of the arc passed through a recessed area in which photoelectric cells had been placed. The passage of the clubhead triggered the cells so that a stroboscopic effect was produced, enabling the user to retain a visual impression of the attitude of the clubhead as it passed through the bottom of the arc. The user, therefore, literally could see whether his swing at impact was outside in, inside out or on the intended line. Further, the device measured clubhead speed translated into the distance the ball would have traveled when hit with that swing. Luis, moreover, had worked out the physics so that other dials displayed how far off line the ball would have gone if the swing pattern were inside or outside the intended line. It certainly was the product of a pure genius.

It was designed to be collapsed with a configuration something like a large black suitcase so that it was portable. That feature led to an adventure I shared with Luis.

A news item announcing that Lloyd Mangrum and Lew Worsham were going to be in San Francisco for an exhibition match triggered Luis' desire to have a first-rate professional evaluate his device. He called me asking if I could arrange a session with Mangrum and Worsham.

I arranged to do so and Luis and I met in the lobby of the St. Francis Hotel where they were staying. As I approached him in the lobby, I was amused at how perfectly his visage fit the cartoon character concept of the mad scientist carrying a large black suitcase containing his latest invention—plus a golf club.

When we arrived at the room and Worsham opened the door, I caught a glimpse of Mangrum leaving the card table where they had been playing cards and positioning himself on his back on the bed with his eyes closed. As we came into the room, he did open one eye which seemed to confirm his predilection that he was being visited by a couple of nuts. Worsham's response to this scene was more hospitable, and he sat on the edge of the bed wondering how the scene was going to play out.

Luis proceeded to open up the black box and explain how the device was designed to work, and then undertook to demonstrate. It can charitably be recorded that Luis' golf swing was not free from flaws and had an awkward character to it that gave additional dimensions to the visage of the mad scientist. The scene, therefore, took on some elements of the bizarre.

Nonetheless, the device performed. The photoelectric cells emitted flashes of light and the needles on the dials spun recording how far and how far off line that swing would have propelled the ball. That performance got Worsham off the bed to take a closer look and got one of Mangrum's eyes open briefly.

Worsham then mounted the platform and took a swing activating the light flashes and the spinning dials. The experience evoked a suggestion that Mangrum have a look at it. While that opened both of Mangrum's eyes, he did not otherwise manifest any interest and it was clear that we had plumbed the depths of Worsham's interest as well.

That experience did not deter Luis from creating a duplicate of the device and arranging to have it delivered to the White House to provide then-President Eisenhower with a facility for improving his game while attending to the affairs of state. It is engaging to visualize the figure of that President somewhere in the White House standing on that platform swinging a club and activating those lights and dials.

Bill Campbell

The golden age of amateur golf reached its climax in 1930 when Bobby Jones retired after accomplishing the "grand slam." While players such as Johnny Goodman, Francis Ouimet, Lawson Little and Charley Yates enlivened the Amateur scene for a while, two developments combined to thin the ranks of first-rate amateur golfers and diminish public interest in the amateur game. One was the emergence of professional golf fueled by increasing amounts of money, the other was the related lamentable evolution of college golf into a professional golf farm system.

While Harvie Ward emerged as an amateur in the post-World War II period as a significant national player and the scene was enlivened for a time by the likes of Charlie Coe and Billy Joe Patton, significant amateur careers became fewer and farther between.

There was—and is—one exception to this deteriorating scene, namely Bill Campbell. All factors in his extraordinary career considered, Bill has to have had the most important and impressive career of any amateur golfer since Bobby Jones. In some respects, moreover, Bill's career transcended Jones.'

Bill is a quintessential amateur. He always has played the game strictly for the love of it while raising a family, developing a business and playing a significant role in an extraordinary variety of ways in his community, including having served in his state's legislature.

His golf-related record qualifies as unique:
- Winner of the U.S. Amateur in 1964
- Finalist in the British Amateur Championship in 1965
- Winner of the U.S. Senior Amateur in 1979 and 1980
- Four-time North and South Amateur champion—1950, 1953, 1957, 1967

- Eight-time U.S. Walker Cup Team Member—1951, 1953, 1955, 1957, 1965, 1967, 1971, 1975; Captain of U.S. Team in 1955.
- Qualified for the U.S. Amateur 37 times, the first in 1938 at age 15.
- Qualified to play in 15 U.S. Opens and 18 Masters.
- Winner of the Men's Amateur in his native West Virginia 15 times.

When you add to all of that his having served as President of the United States Golf Association and as Captain of the Royal and Ancient Golf Club of St. Andrews, surely unique becomes a somewhat inadequate description of such an amateur career.

What gives all of that further substance are his character and characteristics. He is a consummate gentleman. His dignified bearing tends to disguise a warm, friendly, sensitive, engaging personality embellished by intelligence.

As he moves gracefully into his 70s, he still is an impressively accomplished player. While the aura is not of his making, but rather is in the eye of the beholder, in the rounds of golf I have been privileged to play with him I have found the combination of the foregoing facts and factors awesome.

I treasure my friendship with him, for which I have golf to thank.

Alistair Cooke

In view of golf's extraordinary appeal, it is not surprising that it attracts extraordinary people. Among the many to whom my involvement in golf has caused me to be introduced, Alistair Cooke has few, if any, peers.

His career in journalism spans considerably more than half a century and encompasses print, radio and television. His radio program, "Letter From America," has run weekly since 1946 and is heard in 52 countries. He continues to broadcast it to millions of people around the world. His "America" television series was a brilliant exposition of this country, its people and its history. Its production was a wonderful product of the breadth and depth of his knowledge and understanding of all of the elements that constitute America. That series was followed by a book he authored on the same subject. Among the many other books he has written are *Generation on Trial* about the Alger Hiss trials, *Six Men* (Charlie Chaplin, Adlai Stevenson, Humphrey Bogart, Edward VIII, H. L. Mencken and Bertrand Russell), each of whom he had encountered in his rich life, and most recently *Fun and Games and Other Amusements*, a collection of newspaper pieces he has written on sporting events and a remarkable array of other amusements. His "Omnibus" television program was a pioneer in creative use of that medium. More recently he hosted "Masterpiece Theater" in a way that set that engaging program in a class by itself. The activities identified above are not meant to be inclusive. They are simply illustrative of a creative and productive career that has dimensions that qualify it as unique.

In view of the extent and intensity of his activities, it is not surprising that he was middle-aged before he discovered golf. It is also not surprising that he took to it with insatiable enthusiasm.

That enthusiasm stimulated a number of observations about the game that have what I identify as special Cooke quality. A couple of examples serve to illustrate:

"The Scots say that Nature itself dictated that golf should be played by the seashore. Rather, the Scots saw in the eroded seacoasts a cheap battleground on which they could whip their fellow man in a game based on the Calvinist doctrine that man is meant to suffer here below and never more than when he goes out to enjoy himself."

When Winston Churchill was a young man he decided to accomplish golf and thought that devoting a part of a summer would be sufficient. The effort, however, was an abysmal failure, which was predictable, because "Winston Churchill, of all people, was not willing to suffer frequent displays of public humiliation."

I met Alistair many years ago when a friend asked me to join himself and a guest for a game. The guest was Alistair. From that meeting evolved a friendship which has provided me with wonderful experiences with him both on and off the golf course.

Those on the golf course have been stimulated by his enthusiasm, which is totally unaffected by how seldom he hits a good golf shot. He provides a splendid example of how to play the game for all the joy that can come from it without regard to the results.

As he approached and then passed ninety years old, the project of getting the ball airborne became increasingly challenging. There was no diminution, however, in how much pleasure he took from the effort and added to that of those who played with him.

When the project was no longer manageable he took solace in quoting P. G. Wodehouse, "Having on this day passed my ninety-second birthday, I find myself overcome by a feeling of peace—a peace which the Rev. P. G. Wodehouse described as 'the peace which passeth all understanding, the peace of a man who has given up golf'."

He had a close friend, Paul Mannheim, with like ability—or rather inability—and, nonetheless, similar enthusiasm for playing the game. I shared a round with the two of them on a cold, windy day at Pebble Beach. Pebble Beach on a windless day would, to put it mildly, have been a serious challenge for each of them. The cold wind that was blowing that day would have posed a serious challenge for Ben Hogan in his prime. Nonetheless, they persevered and, with only modest departures from the rules, somehow managed to finish all 18 holes. A computer would have been needed to record their scores. Their respective enthusiasms, however, were unaffected. For example, there is a road which runs alongside the 16th hole which makes a sharp right turn about 50 yards from the tee. Paul's driver swing produced a slice of such dimensions that the ball followed the contour of the road. As Paul contemplated its errant route he said, "Well at least it is in the right-hand lane."

Shortly after that adventure I was having a drink with Paul and his wife. When Paul left the room I recounted that incident on the 16th tee. Mrs. Mannheim's response was a comment about how she resisted walking around with him while he played because it was too painful to have to witness such a succession of awful golf shots. On one occasion when he had persuaded her to join him, one of his terrible shots caused her to exclaim, "Oh Paul, how could you!" His immediate response was to say "What do you expect after 2,000 years of persecution!"

Those experiences off the golf course have been enriched by Alistair's encyclopedic memory. He has had personal exposure to virtually everyone who has had an impact on life in this country in the last seventy years. That memory, that knowledge, that exposure and his extraordinary facility to put memories, thoughts and observations into words make evenings spent with him memorable, to say the least.

Sean Connery

Given the verve, imagination, courage, athleticism and sheer audaciousness he manifests, you have to know that James Bond is a golfer. While there have been a lot of imitators, there has only been one genuine James Bond and that, of course, is Sean Connery. When you consider the character and characteristics that Sean identified in James Bond, obviously Sean would have to be a golfer and indeed, he is.

It is a cliche that if you want to get the true measure of the person, simply play a game of golf with him or her. Like most cliches, that one expresses an essential truism. Playing a game of golf with Sean simply confirms that the character and characteristics he imparted to James Bond were substantially his own and they include unbridled enthusiasm and intense competitiveness. As you would expect, he plays exceptionally well.

Sean has a single digit handicap, which reflects consistent skill with all the clubs and shots. As a member of the Royal and Ancient Golf Club of St. Andrews he has won the club's Jubilee Vase.

After a spirited game enjoyed with him recently, my wife and I spent a delightful evening with him embellished by some appropriately good wine and a leisurely meal. However much may have been written about his personal history, his recounting of it in the course of that evening is worth repeating.

He came from a very poor family living in an Edinburgh ghetto with precious little effective education. He was on his own as a youngster and scratched out a living doing odd jobs until his athleticism secured a job as a professional football (i.e., in American parlance, soccer) player. After some time in that role, he learned of an opening in the company doing the musical "South Pacific." His adventurous spirit and athleticism projected him into that unlikely role.

After he had been appearing in the South Pacific for some time, someone saw in him potential for becoming an actor and suggested that he pursue that prospect. His immediate response was that that did not make any sense, because he was so uneducated and had such a thick Scottish brogue that if he were to develop any thespian skills, very few people would be able to understand him. He became convinced, nonetheless, that attempting to overcome those obstacles was worth the effort. He was given a long list of books to read, including those written by the great Russian, British, Irish and American authors and he also acquired a tape machine, which in those days was awkwardly large, and tapes containing dialogue expressed with an acceptable English accent.

As he traveled with the South Pacific company, he spent every waking minute off the stage either in the library or listening to the tapes. The monumental effort paid off in a self-acquired education which is impressive and an accent which is not only acceptable, but which has a distinctive quality.

That achievement led to a broad variety of roles at various levels of theater. One day he heard that a producer was preparing to produce a movie based upon an Ian Fleming novel and was holding auditions to identify the actor to play the James Bond role. He pursued that lead to a meeting with the producer in which, acting on a hunch, he declined to audition, taking the position that his experience ought to provide adequate basis for evaluating him. He made the desired impression. The producer wanted Cary Grant for the role, but he could not raise the money and he settled for Sean. The rest is history.

As he has aged and otherwise gone beyond the James Bond role, Sean has succeeded in continuing a career with remarkable dimensions. One of the more impressive elements of that career is that it is carefully structured to accommodate a considerable quantity of quality golf.

Bing Crosby

Bing Crosby's golf swing was a lot like his singing voice—sort of loose and lazy. He applied it to the shot with a combination of grace and nonchalance that added flavor to the process. As in his singing, where apparent casualness masked a consummate professional performing with meticulous care for quality, the casual appearance of his approach to golf masked an intensity of desire to play as well as he could.

He played, moreover, remarkably well and qualified for both the U.S. Amateur and the British Amateur Championships.

The USGA gives qualifiers in the Amateur Championship medals to memorialize that achievement. Bing's medal turned up among his prized possessions after he died. His son, Nathaniel, had it mounted on a chain which he wore around his neck. In the course of winning the U.S. Amateur Championship at The Olympic Club in 1981, Nathaniel frequently touched the medal with the sense that doing so sort of put him in touch with Bing, a sense that Nathaniel found extraordinarily helpful.

I first met Bing in the 1930s at Lakeside Golf Club in southern California where Bing was a member. Given his genial egalitarian nature, I was not surprised to learn that he played a lot of his golf there in the very early mornings with the caddies.

At that time there was a Lakeside member named John Montegue who was a local legend because he hit the ball prodigious distances and otherwise played spectacularly well. Montegue's legendary status was local because he confined his golf to Lakeside and lived reclusively.

The purveyors of the Montegue legend included caddies who swore to having seen him knock a bird off an electricity line with a five iron. One element of the legend that did have a lot of currency among the members was a bet he allegedly made with Bing that he could beat Bing in a one hole match on the 10th hole with Bing having a full complement of clubs and Montegue confined to a baseball bat, a shovel and a rake. According to the legend, Bing made a par four and lost to a birdie three produced by a fungo shot with the bat into the green side sand bunker, followed by a shovel shot onto the green and a putt with a rake into the hole!

As the Montegue legend spread far beyond Lakeside, it caused him to be identified as a fugitive from a murder charge. He was accused of having been involved with some others in a robbery attempt in an upstate New York tavern in which one of the group, not Montegue, shot someone. Fifteen or more years had passed since the incident. A proceeding concerned with the charge was held in a New York court. Bing and Bob Hope and other luminaries appeared as character witnesses for Montegue and he was absolved of the charge.

The resulting publicity led to his playing an exhibition match with Babe Zaharias and Babe Ruth which had to be called off after nine holes because the huge gallery was out of control. Shortly thereafter John Montegue faded from the scene, leaving only the legend.

Playing golf with Bing was a distinct experience. The quality of his play was embellished by his easy going style and the pleasure he so engagingly manifested, for example, by a lot of whistling of popular ballads right on tune between shots.

I was in a threesome with Bing on one of those stunning days at Cypress Point which make the playing of that course such a magical experience. On the 15th hole we were joined by Kathryn, whom he had recently married. She was extraordinarily attractive and embellished by her company the playing of the remaining holes.

As we finished the round, Bing invited me and my host, with whom I was spending the weekend, to join Bing and Kathryn for tea in the clubhouse. Later in the locker room my host said, "You are not going to join those people, are you? He is nothing but a vaudevillian!" I gained two impressions from that incident. One was that my host was a hopeless bigot and the other that there were delightful dimensions to Bing's personality to which Kathryn added a great deal.

The Crosby, which he started as a small gathering of some of his amateur and professional friends at Rancho Santa Fe, became one of the premier events in golf when he moved it to the Monterey Peninsula after WW II. The combination of the format, the courses, the weather (which ranged from the sublime to the ridiculous) and Bing's inimitable presence made playing in The Crosby a unique experience. Dimensions were added to all of that for me when I turned up as the amateur on the winning team and was presented with a huge, beautiful silver trophy by Bing at The Clambake.

Those clambakes in the early years were sensational parties. They were held on Sunday night after the last round. The pros in those years were not taking off for outings or other events and they, along with everyone else involved, turned up for Bing's party. Typically, Bing would have premier performers such as Rosemary Clooney, Phil Harris and Les Brown join him. Bing obviously reveled in that scene and the others performed with related enthusiasm. To say that they were sensational parties only begins to express the full flavor of those experiences.

As the aging process inexorably eroded his skills, he lost none of his enthusiasm for playing the game. The day before he died, he played golf in Spain and wrote a postcard to Alistair Cooke in which he recorded how rotten had been his play that day and added the stirring declaration, "…but I will never surrender!"

That certainly is the battle cry of a true golfer, and that he certainly was.

Bernard Darwin

As mentioned previously, Bernard Darwin may have been the best there has ever been at the art and craft of reporting and commenting on golf. His pieces, written for *The Times* (London), were lyrical essays that did much more than report. They captured the essence of the myriad features that make golf such a fascinating game. I met him while playing golf for Oxford.

He was an extraordinarily good player. He played on the Cambridge Golf Team and in the first Walker Cup Match which was played at the National Golf Links of America in 1922. He may well have developed into a great player, but for a volcanic temper that he had a terrible time trying to control.

An illustration of that temper is worth recounting. He was playing a four ball with some friends at Woking near London. On the first hole, a short four-par, he placed his second shot a few feet from the hole and proceeded to miss the putt. When he serenely accepted that failure, the other players noted how remarkable that was. When he missed an even shorter putt for a birdie on the second hole without any display of emotion, the others were startled. When, on the third, another short birdie putt slid by the hole and the serenity of his composure persisted, the others began to think that they were witness to a miraculous transformation.

On the fourth, a short hole, he struck a majestic iron shot which finished a few feet from the hole. When he missed that putt, there was a moment of his staring in obvious disbelief at the still visible ball, followed by his slowly sinking to his knees, bending over and, with jaw agape, extracting with his teeth a large hunk of turf grass from the green. He then reared back and, with bits of turf dripping down his chin, opened his arms, glared into the stratosphere and shouted, "Now God, have you humiliated me enough?"

There may have been some benefit from that temper which found its way into his writing, because there was real passion for and about the game that was the foundation for his lyrical approach to it.

His favorite course was Aberdovey, an engaging links course in Wales. He wrote about it so often and with such enthusiasm that for any Darwin fan a pilgrimage to play it is a must. My pilgrimage was richly rewarded, because in the playing of it I could relate to his feelings for it.

As I think about him, which I often do, I recall the visage of him when he was covering the match against Cambridge at Royal St. Georges in which I played. He was dressed protected from the elements in an ankle length heavy dark overcoat. He was standing alone on a dune silhouetted against the somber sky. Somehow, for me, there was something majestic in that presence.

Ben Hogan

Any discussion of the residents in the pantheon of golf's all time great players sooner rather than later turns to Ben Hogan.

There certainly are manifold reasons to so identify him. Take, for example, some of the elements of his record:

- In 1946 he played in 32 tournaments and all he did was win 13 of them and finish runner-up in 6;
- In 1947 he won 6 out of 24;
- In 1948 he won 9 out of 24 and was either first, second or third in 15;
- Following the accident in which he was almost killed, he was confined to 4 or 5 events a year. In the four-year period 1950 through 1953, he played in 17 official events and he won 9 including 3 U.S. Opens, 2 Masters and the only British Open in which he ever played.
- In 1953 he only played in 7 events and he won 5 of them including the U.S. Open, the British Open and The Masters.

The record, however incredible, only begins to tell the Hogan story. There is no way to put that story into proper perspective in a few paragraphs. Some elements of it, however, add to the understanding of how extraordinary he was.

In contrast to Sam Snead, who sauntered out of the hills of West Virginia with a golf swing made in heaven, Hogan built his swing piece by piece, overcame a duck hook that almost ended his career before it started and created a golf swing that was exclusively his and sensationally successful by working harder, thinking deeper and analyzing and adapting better perhaps than anyone who ever lived.

He was taciturn almost to the point of being reclusive. He played his friend Jimmy Demaret in the PGA Championship in 1946 and beat him 10 and 9. When Demaret was asked whether Hogan had spoken to him during the course of the match, Demaret replied, "Oh yes, he spoke to me on every hole; when we reached the green, Ben said, 'You're away'."

His game was the prime medium through which he communicated. Watching Ben Hogan play a round of golf was an ultimate experience in witnessing how the game should be played. There was a game plan for every hole that meticulously accounted for all of the characteristics he had identified and the conditions that existed on that hole on that particular day. The thoughtfulness in his approach to each shot translated into real drama. The execution so often was so flawless that watching him play was a deeply emotional experience.

In sum, his game was an art form executed by a consummate artist.

When Hogan came to play in the U.S. Open at the Olympic Club in 1966, the site of his shocking loss to Jack Fleck 11 years earlier, he was well past his prime, but nonetheless a giant presence. A few days before the first round I made a pronouncement to my wife and children to the effect that everyone who was ambulatory, making a total of six, was going to join me in a unique experience; that is, we were going to watch Ben Hogan play a round of golf in the U.S. Open. I emphasized how important it was to be at the first tee when he started and to see every shot we could thereafter.

When the day came, getting such a large group with such an age spread moving in a timely way proved to be more than I could handle. The resulting frustration also was very nearly more than I could handle when, as we finally reached the course, he was teeing off on the second hole and the closest we could get was 250 yards from the tee at a place off the fairway well down the hill where we literally could see nothing but the hill. As I stood there thinking about whether we should move on a ball came bouncing down the hill and came to rest within a few feet of where we were standing. In due course Hogan appeared; he had hit what then was an uncharacteristic hook off the tee.

We then were treated to a typical Hoganesque performance. With a cigarette hanging from his mouth, he analyzed his problem, selected his club, took a last drag on the cigarette, flipped it away and proceeded to hit an absolutely glorious shot into the center of the green (which, of course, we could not see).

When we reached the green area my frustration had only slightly abated when my wife poked me, called my attention to her closed right hand, which she then opened to reveal the butt of Hogan's cigarette. She had retrieved it after his second shot.

The rancor went out of me at that moment. The day developed as I hoped it might and that cigarette butt adorned the bulletin board in our kitchen until it finally disintegrated.

Recently I had an engaging discussion with Ken Venturi regarding Hogan. Ken enjoyed a close personal relationship with Hogan. When I recounted the foregoing experience at Olympic, Ken said, "Do you remember who was playing with Hogan that day?" When I replied that I did not, Ken said it was Ken who was paired with him. Ken went on to recall that shot Hogan hit onto the second green and noted that it finished 12 feet from the hole. Ken said that when Hogan addressed that 12 foot putt, Ben was immobilized for an excruciatingly long time before he stepped away from the ball, walked over to Ken and whispered, "I can't take the putter back!" Ken gave what turned out to be the right response by saying, "Ben, no one gives a ____ !" Hogan's eyes widened considerably before he turned around, walked back to the ball and made a tolerable stroke.

The deterioration of Hogan's putting — to the ultimate degradation of any ability to make any sort of a stroke — is beyond understanding. It certainly is a dramatic illustration of how difficult it is to control the mental element of the game. Ben Hogan has to have been the ultimate example of mind controlling matter and yet, in the end, standing over a putt, his mind could not make his hands move.

I enjoyed the privilege of playing some golf with him — at the course he co-designed in Texas with Joe Lee (The Trophy Club), at Seminole in Florida and at Cypress Point. I should add that I was his partner in a game at Seminole when we lost every bet we made, a distinction I would just as soon forget.

Among the many characteristics he had which profoundly impressed me was the distinct impression he gave that every golf shot he played, regardless of the circumstances, was a privilege which carried with it a commensurate responsibility to apply to that shot every element of his concentration, experience and skill.

That characteristic was a consistent feature of his game. It was also an important part of the last game I played with him, at Cypress Point. His eyesight had so deteriorated that he had to rely on this caddie to give him the hole features and shot distances. Nevertheless, every shot was played with the same meticulous care that he brought to bear in his prime.

Like all great players he had a reverence for the game that was inspiring.

Any retrospective on Ben Hogan's career has to include the 1953 British Open at Carnoustie in Scotland. It was the only British Open in which he ever played. He won it, not just decisively, but with such consummate shot making and resolute course management in difficult conditions that his victory ranks with the more impressive triumphs in the whole history of golf. In fact, it was so spectacular that he was accorded a ticker-tape parade up Broadway in New York on his way home. To this day when you play Carnoustie, it is likely that your caddie will point out to you the four places, each within a few feet of the other, on the dangerous left side of the sixth fairway from which Hogan played his second shot, setting up the four birdies he recorded on that hole.

The games I was privileged to play with him belied Ben's reputation as a dour competitor, because they were indeed friendly and Ben contributed significantly to that atmosphere.

My golf swing has a definitive pause in the transition from the backswing to the downswing. In one of the golf games I enjoyed with Ben I managed on one hole to hit my tee shot beyond his. I hit another solid tee shot from the next tee. When Ben hit his, I noticed that both his turn and his arc increased and his drive, as the saying goes, "airmailed" mine. As we left the tee he turned to me with a twinkle in his eye and said "You know, Sandy, you could hit it a fair piece if you did not stop and visit on the way down."

It was after a game with him at Seminole in Florida that I spent a memorable evening with him, his wife, Valerie, and two friends. I had an opportunity to talk with Valerie while the others were engaged in a separate conversation.

I took that opportunity to discuss the importance of his winning the 1953 British Open at Carnoustie.

In that discussion, Valerie added some remarkable dimensions to the story of that triumph. She said that she had been urging Ben to enter for some time, which he refused to do, saying that he had nothing that he needed to prove by playing and, in view of the post-accident problems he had with circulation in his legs, it made no sense to go to Scotland to suffer in the cold, windy conditions which were likely to occur.

Having failed to persuade him, Valerie entered him. When, some time later, Ben learned that she had done so, he reluctantly agreed to play but continued to express concern about how he would deal with the weather. Valerie reacted to those concerns by acquiring every ointment, medication, wrapping and device she could find which might ameliorate the problem. Her acquisitions added up to quite a pile that accumulated in the bedroom. When Ben focused on the pile he pointed to it and said, "If that goes, I don't go!" Valerie, recognizing that the moment of truth had arrived, responded, "If that does not go, I don't go. Take your choice!"

Ben chose Valerie and the medicaments, and off they went to a championship victory that added the ultimate dimension to Ben's career. They were housed in Scotland in a country estate with a staff of a dozen. A chauffeur-driven Humber was arranged to drive Ben to and from the course.

Valerie recounted the scene at the estate when Ben returned from the final round with the claret jug, riding in the back of the Humber with his caddie and bag in front with the chauffeur. The staff was lined up in the drive to congratulate him. Each of the men stepped forward in turn solemnly to shake his hand and each of the women stepped forward in turn, curtsied and then kissed his cheek. Each man and woman then went to the golf bag and retrieved a good luck amulet each had managed to put in the bag before he left for that final round! Valerie said it was the only time she had ever seen Ben Hogan reduced to tears.

And so it was that one of the more significant performances in the history of golf was accorded an impromptu reception by some servants in Scotland that meant more to Ben Hogan than the ticker-tape parade on Broadway that followed.

Honoring Bob Hope

In the late 1970s the USO staged a television extravaganza in the Kennedy Center in Washington D.C. honoring Bob Hope. Arnold Palmer and I were recruited by the U.S. Army general in charge of the event to make a special presentation to Hope as a part of the program. The plan was to have Arnold and me make Hope an honorary Associate of the United States Golf Association in a ceremony which included presenting Hope with a coat specially made for the occasion.

My role included arranging for the coat, which turned out to be complicated, because getting an accurate read on Hope's coat size was, to put it mildly, not easy. The time consumed in doing so created a problem of having the coat made and delivered in time for the ceremony. That involved dispatching a USGA executive to the tailor in New York to pick up the coat, fly to Washington and deliver it to me at the airport when I arrived from San Francisco just in time to make it to the Kennedy Center at the appointed hour.

And so it was that, somewhat breathless, I made it to the check-in desk at the Kennedy Center carrying the coat on a hanger and working into my thespian mode suitable for an appearance on national television with Arnold Palmer and Bob Hope.

Unfortunately, however, the young lady at the desk had never heard of me or any such part of the program and my name was not on her list of participants. My effort to rectify the situation was complicated by the apparent perception that I was some kind of a nut carrying a coat on a hanger trying to inject myself into the program. That perception, I believe, was shared by everyone of the considerable number of people I managed to involve in the problem as my frustration developed into potentially pyrotechnic anger.

At the point when I thought the police were going to be called to take me away, someone appeared from some inner sanctum with the explanation that Arnold Palmer's plans had been changed so that Arnold could not be there and, therefore, that part of the program had been eliminated.

I took precious little satisfaction from being relieved of the perception that I was some kind of nut. My only recourse was to return to the airport still carrying the coat and take the next available plane back to San Francisco. I did, however, derive some satisfaction by devoting most of the flight back to a letter to the general expressing my view of his operation and my gratitude for his not having been given a military command putting people's lives at risk.

Bobby Jones

Every sport has its performers who not only were the best during the years of their triumphs, but are ranked among the best of the best so as to be in the pantheon of the sport's acknowledged heroes. The sport of golf has the distinction of developing heroes with the character and characteristics identifying them as exemplary human beings with a good deal to offer beyond their playing abilities.

You can, I think, go back to Old Tom Morris to prove that point. In this century, you have Harry Vardon, Francis Ouimet, Walter Hagen, Bobby Jones, Byron Nelson, Ben Hogan, Arnold Palmer, Jack Nicklaus, Tom Watson and Tiger Woods.

Perhaps the most extraordinary person in that lineup was Bobby Jones. He was intensely competitive. No one, of course, reaches the pinnacle of any game without having that characteristic to an extraordinary degree. Jones' competitive nature certainly was acute. For example, during a championship, he could only manage to eat and to hold down benign foods such as tea and dried toast. One of the factors that made him so distinctive, however, was that however intensely he wanted to win, he managed to play the game with such grace and charm that he may have been the most appealing personality to achieve pre-eminence in any sport. That distinction takes on added dimensions when you consider that he had to overcome a temper that at times became literally uncontrollable.

He was a consummate sportsman. He and Al Espinosa tied for the United States Open Championship after the regulation 72 holes at Winged Foot in 1929. At that time the playoffs were conducted over 36 holes. Jones persuaded the USGA to delay the start of the playoffs so that Espinosa, who was a

Catholic, would have time comfortably to go to mass before the playoff started. It should also be noted that Jones then proceeded to beat Espinosa by 23 strokes.

There was an experience at the Old Course in St. Andrews that illustrates how remarkably attractive he was. It was in 1936, six years after he had retired from competitive golf. He and some friends were staying for a few days at Gleneagles in Scotland while en route to the Olympic Games in Berlin. Bobby (he preferred to be called Bob, but the media and his legions of fans preferred Bobby) had a spontaneous desire to have a round of golf on the Old Course. No one but the starter, the caddies and a few R&A members knew he was there when he drove from the first tee starting a friendly round with three of his friends. The news, however, that Bobby Jones was playing the Old Course went through the community as if by telepathy. He had only played a few holes before a large crowd was following him. The crowd rapidly grew as activity in the old gray town practically shut down so that it numbered in the thousands (estimated at six thousand) by the time he reached the second nine. The flavor of the occasion stimulated him to rise to it. He produced a splendid 68, reviving wonderful memories for all who saw it of how graceful and charming the game can be when played by the likes of Bobby Jones.

It was in that setting that a young Scot carrying Jones' bag witnessing a shot that Jones had played was moved to say "My, but you are a wonder, Sir!" And indeed he was.

He came back to St. Andrews in 1958 as the Captain of the team of American amateurs playing for the Eisenhower Trophy (an event that came to be known as the World Amateur Team Championship). The town elders used the occasion to make him an honorary citizen of the town, an honor accorded only one other person, Benjamin Franklin.

Bobby accepted the honor with a performance characterized by the sort of grace and charm that made his play so distinctive. He had prepared a speech, but was so moved by the occasion that he discarded his text and simply spoke extemporaneously from his heart. In that setting he said that he could take out of his life all of the experiences he had had, excepting only those at St. Andrews, and he would have lived a very full life indeed. Those who witnessed that performance will never forget it.

After he died in December 1971 from the terrible disease that so afflicted and crippled him for so many years, there was a memorial service conducted in the same kirk in which the honorary citizen ceremony had been performed. The eulogy was spoken by Roger Wethered, whom Bobby had beaten in the final of the British Amateur Championship in 1930 on the Old Course, providing one of the four titles constituting "The Grand Slam." It was a perfectly beautiful service, reviving memories of him and honoring the giant of a man who had set a standard for embellishing of the playing the game with elements of grace and charm that will live through the ages.

Jones added considerably to the legend that he became and to the game that he loved so passionately by writing fulsomely with a lucid and engaging style that made it a pleasure to read his books and articles.

It is certainly fitting, therefore, that the most prestigious award a golfer can be given in this country is the Bob Jones Award made annually by the United States Golf Association. It is also fitting that a golf course that is so excellent and beautiful as is Augusta National, and a golf tournament that is such an exemplary showcase for the game of golf as is The Masters, each was the creation of Bobby Jones.

Much more can and should be said about him. Suffice it to say here, however, that he and the others I have identified serve as useful examples of one of golf's distinctive features, which is that it takes character to play the game properly and it takes special character to excel at it. It is no accident, therefore, but it is rather the logical result of that feature, that those who have resided at the pinnacle of the game of golf have also been engaging and effective human beings.

While I only saw him play once, he had a profound influence on my life. That was so, even though my exposure to him, except for the round I saw him play at Wilshire Country Club, was confined to the print media. Nonetheless, as a very young boy, I recognized qualities of grace, charm, integrity, competitive fire and a capacity to articulate that impressed me and made we want to emulate them. To illustrate how early that influence shaped me, when Jones lost to George von Elm in the finals of the U.S. Amateur in 1926, I was seriously upset—at the age of 6.

I did also, in a sense, share an extraordinary experience with him. It occurred in 1936 following his round at St. Andrews, when Jones was at the Berlin

Olympic Games. I also attended those Olympics and was a witness, as was Jones, to what I submit was and is the greatest athletic performance of all time. The setting was Berlin's Olympic Stadium. The principals were Adolf Hitler and Jesse Owens. The witnesses, in addition to Jones and me, were approximately 75,000 Germans, 20,000 Europeans and 5,000 Americans.

The background for the particular performance was the Nazi view of the human race as stratified, with the Aryans supremely placed at the top and the Africans (i.e. blacks) securely mired at the bottom.

The construct of the Stadium had a throne-like structure for Hitler consisting of a platform and a throne chair located mid-stadium at about the 10th row. The empty chair on that platform was an eye-catcher as people entered the stadium. Every afternoon exactly at 4 o'clock Hitler would arrive and position himself standing in front of that chair. That appearance moved the 75,000 Germans into a virtual frenzy of Nazi saluting and shouts of "seig heil" that went on each day for about 15 minutes. Even the 16-year-old boy that I was recognized something ominous in that form of adulation.

It was poetic justice that U.S. Olympic Team was the first from this country that was dominated by African-American athletes so that Hitler suffered the discomfort of having to watch a wonderful lot of black chests break tapes while the Aryans figuratively were eating their cinders.

Those results also posed a special problem for Hitler, because it was arranged for gold-medal winners to cap the victory-stand honor with the ultimate honor of being escorted to the throne and personally congratulated by der Fuhrer himself. The supremacy nonsense, however, precluded African Americans from being so honored.

Preeminent among American athletes was Jesse Owens, who was the dominant figure of those games. Before the games concluded with the long jump, Owens had won three gold medals—the 100 meters, 200 meters and as anchor of the 100 x 4 meter relay. He had, therefore, been precluded from three Hitlerian accolades.

In the long jump he made the longest jump in the qualifying rounds. The protocol then was that he did not have to jump again unless and until someone jumped farther. It developed that on his final jump a German went farther than he had ever jumped before and farther than the Owens jump.

55

Owens had three jumps remaining.

At that point all track and field events but the long jump had concluded. Owens was the only person moving in that vast stadium. His skin color was accentuated by the white track suit and the white shoes he wore. As he prepared to start down the runway for his first of those three jumps, the 75,000 Germans began to whistle, which I interpreted as their form of catcall. When Owens reached the take-off board he crowhopped (i.e., took off with part of his foot beyond the pit edge of the board) so that the jump was disqualified. That development added to the volume and shrillness of the whistling.

On his second attempt, he lost his step so that he distressingly ran through the pit. What the Germans presumed they were seeing, therefore, at long last, was a black man having to deal with an Aryan he could not handle. The whistling became almost deafening as Owens carefully retraced his steps, took a long look into the pit, apparently focusing on where he needed to land, and then with excruciating deliberation positioned himself ready to start his run.

This time he hit the board perfectly and took off so that he was suspended in space until he came down at a distance that surpassed the German's mark and established a new world's record!

If ever an athlete has surmounted each pressure in such excruciatingly difficult circumstances with such a world record performance, I certainly have neither seen nor heard of it.

In view of my perceptions of who and what Bobby Jones was and what he had accomplished, it seems specially right that, in a sense, I should have experienced all that with him.

Hank Ketcham

Hank was the creator of Dennis the Menace. He applied his creativity to a broad spectrum of activity. Having taken the artistry in the Dennis cartoons to the limits of that form of expression, he turned to oil painting. As he was accomplishing that form of artistic expression, he grew a beard, which moved me to identify him in my flawless French pronunciation as "Henri."

As has so often been the case in the life I have been privileged to live, Hank is one of those extraordinary people I have met in the context of playing golf. He was a member of Cypress Point where I also am privileged to be a member. As a 10 handicap golfer, Hank played more than respectfully. For a number of years he was paired in the The Crosby with Charles Shultz, the creator of Peanuts. There was something specially engaging to observe those two wonderfully creative people, whose creativity had enlivened so many lives in so many ways, happily pursuing The Grail that is the game.

Hank and I enjoyed a special relationship nurtured by our love affairs with the game. The relationship's special quality led to our arranging annually to play together at Cypress Point on the last day of each year. It was a way of expressing, each to the other, the appreciation felt for the times we had enjoyed together in the year we were now bringing to a close.

I have enjoyed a wonderful lot of golf with him. His enthusiasm for life generally got focused in his enthusiasm for playing golf. Furthermore, Hank saw the world through his own special prism. There was a humorous tint that showed up in all facets of that prism and was delightfully manifest in the course of a round of golf with him. Hank was involved in the adventure with Tom Watson and in the "chip in" both described on page 82.

I was playing with Hank when I struck a shot on a three-par hole that ended up as my second hole-in-one, 58 years after my first hole-in-one. Hank seized on that interval as the product of my having been so upset by all of the root beer that I had to buy on the occasion of my first hole-in-one when I was 11 years old that I had assiduously avoided making another.

When I think of the games of golf that I have suffered with people who take themselves and the game too seriously, I am especially grateful for all of the delightful experiences that I have been privileged to share on golf courses with Hank Ketcham.

Hank has moved on (as I prefer to think about it), hopefully into a world where Dennis will reconnect with Mr. and Mrs. Wilson. Each of us whose lives he touched will have had them enriched by such a blithe spirit who engaged us so endearingly.

Tony Lema

Occasionally, all too occasionally, someone develops as a golfer with more to add to the golf scene than his extraordinary skill. Jimmy Demaret was such a person. So also was Tony Lema. Tony's golf swing had a special rhythm that created the impression that the clubhead simply flowed into the ball. That swing and the consummate skill with which he used it would have distinguished Tony regardless of his personality. Tony, however, was not just eminently likable. He was a free spirit who lived life with a special flair.

His swing and skill produced a British Open victory on the Old Course in 1964. His flair produced the sobriquet "Champagne Tony" because he celebrated his first PGA Tour event victory by providing the press corps with champagne and he continued to provide those celebrations for all his subsequent victories.

A brilliant career embellished by a wonderfully free spirit was truncated by a tragic airplane accident in 1966.

I had the privilege of presiding at Tony's posthumous induction into the Bay Area Sports Hall of Fame in 2000. I did so as follows:

> There was much more to the champagne label that Tony enjoyed than identifying his past victory parties. It served to identify an effervescent personality that added classy luster to any scene in which he played a part.
>
> That label was not the product of some publicity gimmick. It evolved from a delightfully spontaneous disposition Tony had to share.
>
> It says a great deal about someone that 34 years after his death you continue to miss him and fervently wish he were here with us tonight. It

is warming to think how much his presence would add to this occasion.

There is a tale to tell which underlies that first post-victory champagne party and says a good deal about how people related to Tony. He won that tournament—his first win in an official PGA event—in a playoff with Bob Rosburg.

Bob vividly recalls that playoff, including Tony's telling him before the last round that if Tony could not win this one he might give up the tour. They tied the first two sudden-death holes with birdies. Tony made a third straight birdie on the next hole to win and inaugurate the legend of champagne Tony Lema. At the time, Rosburg classified Tony's birdie on the first hole as a miracle, because Tony so hooked his tee shot that Rossie was sure it would be out of bounds; miraculously, the ball was found just barely in bounds.

Twenty-five years later, Rosburg was playing in a senior event when he was approached by a man in the gallery who asked Bob if he remembered that playoff. Assured that Bob did, the man went on to say "that tee shot Tony hit off the first tee went out of bounds, but I kicked it back in. I had had a few beers, Tony and I were both ex-marines, he was such a great guy and I was rooting so hard for him I just had to kick that ball back in bounds." Now those of you who know Rossie will understand that the passage of 25 years would not take any edge off how much he hated to lose and how outraged he would be over some beered-up spectator stealing the win from him. So Rossie glared at the guy and said, "if you hadn't kicked that ball back in, Tony might still be alive."

That leads to the thought of how much the current sports scene, especially golf, needs a Tony Lema. Just imagine how much would have been added to the lore of the game if he had been there playing it over these past three decades! Tony was a consummate lover. He loved life and he loved the game he played.

That love goes back a long way. As a youngster helping his widowed mother support the family, Tony worked the night shift in a cannery so he could play golf during the day.

His book "Golfers Gold" provides a perspective on the game he so loved which says a lot about Tony and about golf; Tony wrote:

"I guess a few no-talent actresses have gotten good parts because the producer had the hots for them. I guess a few good baseball players never got a real chance to show their wares because the manager could not stand them. I guess a few quarterbacks were made to look bad because their teammates wouldn't block for them. I guess a few junior executives became senior executives because they could play office politics. Well, you can't win golf tournaments by playing politics. Once you have put your ball down on the first tee no one can hold you back but yourself."

It took death to hold back Tony Lema, but the memory of him makes him a living legend who enriched his time and the game he loved and who richly deserves the honor being accorded him here tonight.

Although we have been deprived of the presence of Tony here with us tonight, we can be grateful for having someone whose consummate courage and resonant love were the prime factors in all Tony Lema became.

And now, ladies and gentlemen, it is my privilege and pleasure to present to you for induction into the Bay Area Sports Hall of Fame, Tony Lema. And to present the award to his mother, Clothilda Lema. Ladies and gentlemen, Mrs. Lema.

Mark McCormack
and Charles Schwab

Golf has provided the setting in which I have become friends respectively with these two extraordinary people. They are combined here because each has the distinction of rare creativity which in one case has created an industry and the other has transformed one.

Mark McCormack as a young lawyer working in a large Cleveland law firm had the entrepreneurial vision, stimulated by a relationship with Arnold Palmer, to see how sports, sports personalities and sports events could be promoted and managed to develop multiple sources of revenue. He was the pioneer in developing what has become a worldwide, multibillion-dollar industry. As his career evolved, he expanded his activity well beyond the world of sports into representing artists, symphony orchestras and conductors, models and such diverse clients as the Vatican and the foundation dispensing the Nobel prizes. This is only an illustrative sample of the scope and diversity of his enterprise.

It was golf that gave all this creativity its initial impetus. Mark was a very good golfer—good enough to qualify for the U.S. Amateur Championship and the U.S. Open Championship. It was in the context of golf where he met Arnold Palmer. The history of what evolved from that meeting is a case study of how vision, energy, intelligence and entrepreneurial spirit figuratively can create and then move mountains.

Mark's approach to life has a focus on what can be described as the big picture. A golf outing with him, therefore, becomes an odyssey. Characteristically that was the identification he gave an outing he arranged with me, Colin Maclaine, a past captain of the R&A and Michael Bonallack, past secretary and captain of the R&A and the winner of five British Amateur Championships. Our venues were Pine Valley, Augusta National, Bay Hill and Isleworth. It was golf on the grand scale and in the grand manner enjoyed with some engagingly extraordinary people.

Consistent with the characteristics of most true lovers of the game, Mark is a remarkably interesting and engaging person. He thoroughly enjoys the good life he has created for himself and he shares that enjoyment with his friends so as also to enhance their lives.

Charles (a.k.a. Chuck) Schwab provides another case study of what imagination, energy and courage can combine to produce. Chuck took the financial services industry, particularly that involved with stock brokerage, and transformed it. He created an organization that could provide those services so much more efficiently and economically that an industry, mired in the status quo, was profoundly changed. The impact of his creativity includes adding countless investors to the capital markets and adding significantly to the vitality of those markets.

Chuck has had to overcome the handicap of dyslexia. It is remarkable how many extraordinarily effective people suffer with that handicap. Perhaps the discipline and perseverance required to deal with it add to their capacity to deal with other challenges.

When you meet people who are spectacularly successful, whose success has included a high public profile and that involves a significant contribution to the community, you do not expect them to be self-effacing. Among the characteristics that make Chuck such an attractive person is the equanimity with which he has dealt with such success.

Chuck also is a remarkably interesting and engaging person. He plays golf extraordinarily well, having been a teammate of Al Geiberger in high school. As is so often true of specially creative people, he plays the game with a combination of intensity, enthusiasm and appreciation for its values so as to make playing with him a distinct experience.

His self-effacing manner belies a capacity to accomplish the seemingly impossible. Recently, when a flawed planning process threatened to turn the first hole of the historic Stanford University golf course into faculty housing and no one involved in the planning was listening to the cries of anguish coming from Stanford's golf community, I enlisted Chuck in the cause. He opened the doors and the minds so that we preserved a priceless piece of golf ground.

He has been a principal in creating wonderful golf courses in Montana, Texas and Hawaii, each of which manifests his love of the game.

Sam Morse,
Pebble Beach and
Cypress Point

Samuel F. B. Morse (a.k.a. Sam; a.k.a. The Duke of Monterey) was the name-sake of his ancestor who invented wireless communication. While Sam Morse's creativity did not shape humanity with the effect of that of his ancestor, he certainly had an impact which was important and enduring.

He turned up on the Monterey Peninsula in 1915, having graduated from Yale where he was Captain of the football team. He responded to Horace Greeley's admonition to "Go west, young man." He had the verve and the imagination to find the financing to acquire approximately 5,500 acres of stunningly beautiful property. It came to be known as "The Del Monte Forest" and included one of the most sensational stretches of coastline imaginable.

When he acquired the property, he acquired a plan developed by the prior owner to subdivide in 80-foot wide lots fronting on Carmel Bay starting from the location of Pebble Beach's 18th green and continuing to the site of the present 10th green.

The fact that he abandoned that plan and made golf the prime factor in his development plan qualifies him as a seer when you consider:

- only a few years had elapsed since Francis Ouimet in 1913 had put golf, for one day, on the front pages of newspaper sports sections;
- an insignificant proportion of the population in this country played golf;
- the concept of making golf a key element in resort/real estate development was virtually unprecedented; and
- Sam Morse had no background in the game. Further-

more, to be charitable, he was a less than adequate
golfer. The golf game that I played with him at Cypress
Point added considerably to my wonder that he had,
in effect, bet the success of his development on the
playing of the game of golf.

Having made that bet he proceeded with prodigious energy, vision and
effectiveness to see to it that it paid off. He employed two amateur golfers, Jack
Neville and Douglas Grant, to design the Pebble Beach golf course. Their glorious creation was embellished by refinements (i.e., converting the 18th hole
from a four par to a landmark five par) provided by another amateur golfer, H.
Chandler Egan.

Egan's work was done to prepare the course for the 1929 U.S. Amateur
Championship. It says a lot for Sam Morse's salesmanship that he persuaded
the USGA to bring that championship to Pebble Beach only ten years after the
course had opened for play. Until them, the Amateur had never been played
west of the Mississippi. Virtually all of the field had to take several days to get
to the Pebble Beach site.

That Championship was a watershed. It established Pebble Beach as one
of the world's premier golf courses. In the year before he achieved the "Grand
Slam" Bobby Jones was defeated in the first round by Johnny Goodman. That
defeat freed up the rest of the week for Jones, who used a good deal of the free
time playing Cypress Point, where he was exposed to the genius of Alister
Mackenzie. Jones, therefore, involved MacKenzie with him in the design of
Augusta National.

Cypress Point was — and is — yet another manifestation of Sam Morse's
vision. There may be a more beautiful landscape on which to lay out a golf
course, but if there is I have not seen it. Sam had the inspiration to give Alister
Mackenzie the project of laying a golf course into that landscape. Mackenzie
had the wit and sensitivity to adapt the course to fit perfectly into that land and
seascape. In doing so he ignored convention by designing three five-pars in the
first six holes, two of them back-to-back, and two three-pars, 15 and 16, also
back-to-back. Along the way he created a masterpiece, "The Sistine Chapel of
Golf."

One way of identifying how matchless is the experience of Cypress Point is how often the course is named by players asked to identify the one course they would play if they were confined to just one for the rest of their lives.

My own experience with the course goes back to 1936 when I played it for the first time. I have been privileged to play it since well over a thousand times. I never drive into the forest surrounding the course anticipating a round there without a jolt of adrenaline from the realization that I am going to be privileged to have another adventure playing Cypress Point.

The development of the club has an extraordinary history. Sam Morse provided the club with that priceless piece of property for a fraction of its value. The stated purchase price was $150,000, which was little enough; it was made more modest by being structured as an option to acquire the title with $50,000 payable in five years and the remainder in 10 years.

The remainder of the development budget was as follows:

Clubhouse	$150,000
Construction of the golf course	$150,000
Incidental items	$ 50,000

The course construction in fact cost $121,000, including Alister Mackenzie's fee. The cost of construction of the Clubhouse was $54,711.

The club's organizers set a target of 250 members who would pay $2,000 each. The effort to so finance the club was started in 1927. One hundred and three members eventually joined at that price. Shortly thereafter the stock market collapsed, followed by what is properly denominated as the Great Depression, with "Great" usable interchangeably with "awful" or "gruesome." By 1933 the membership had shrunk to 45.

As the numbers of members declined and the money dried up, Sam Morse provided what was needed to keep Cypress Point operating. By 1938 there were just 34 members. Sam hung on to these by reducing the dues to $10 a month and providing each with free access to both the Pebble Beach course and lodge.

During World War II the club shut down completely for 18 months. When it reopened and the economy improved, the membership slowly increased until it became economically viable.

While the club controls initiation fees and keeps them at a relatively modest level, in terms of having access to just about the most beautiful and exhilarating experiences golf can provide, membership in the club is practically priceless.

Sam Morse certainly provided the world, and especially the world of golf, with a monumental legacy. Pebble Beach and Cypress Point are enduring monuments to a giant of a man with a vision to match.

Byron Nelson

As we think about the great players whose careers have been tributes to the game, Byron Nelson immediately comes to mind. His record of 11 straight Tour wins in 1945 has to be the most unbeatable record in all of sport.

One word comes closest to capturing the essence of Byron Nelson, and that is quality. His golf game was pure quality and in all respects, he was, and happily still is, a quality person.

His dream of owning a cattle ranch having been realized out of his money winnings, he retired from sustained competitive golf while still in his prime. If he had continued his competitive career, he could have challenged Jack Nicklaus for the identity of best of all time.

He came from a family of modest means and worked his way into the game as a caddie. Notwithstanding his spectacular success as a golfer, he never lost his modest, unassuming demeanor. He played the game, however, with a style so graceful as to be poetic and he came to be known as Lord Byron.

His friendship with Ben Hogan was formed when they were boys sharing the experience of caddying at a local club. As their careers evolved, they remained close friends. Hogan's early career was affected by a persistent hook (he has been heard to say that when he hit a hook, he wanted to throw up). In 1939 the Hogans visited the Nelsons for five days, during which Ben and Byron practiced together. Hogan's antidote for the hook was to play with an open-faced driver. Byron was convinced that doing so aggravated the hook problem, because viewing the open face at address caused a tendency to close it coming into the ball. Byron, therefore, produced a driver from his shop which had a slightly closed face and persuaded Ben to try it. Ben did so with stunning results so that, as Byron puts it, Ben used it until he wore off the sole plate.

Byron's disposition to use his gift for playing the game to enhance the lives and careers of others has included Tom Watson among its beneficiaries. As Tom struggled early in his career, Byron expressed interest in helping him. While the help proved to be beneficial, more important has been the friendship that evolved and meant so much to Tom.

Like all truly great players, Byron has had a lifelong passionate affair with the game. One manifestation of that love was his desire to help others excel at it. I recently experienced another example that is worth recording. He has suffered with a hip problem, which prevents him from making any turn and confines him to hitting the ball entirely with his hands. I had the privilege of playing golf with him. But for the way that Byron dealt with his problems, it would have been distressing to see one of the game's all-time great players confined to a golf cart and to the puny distances he could manage to hit the ball with his hands. As it evolved, however, the game was memorably enjoyable, because Byron managed to take such pleasure out of making the best of what he could do with what he had to work with that day and out of the good shots that the rest of us occasionally produced.

It was heartwarming to realize that a hero had retained his heroic qualities long after his skills had left him. He certainly still is Lord Byron.

Major James Nesmeth

The game of golf has produced a lot of sagas that are loaded with drama. Take, for example, Gene Sarazen holing a four wood shot for a double eagle on 15 at Augusta to enable him to tie Craig Wood and go on to win The Masters in a playoff. While such exploits have continued to command attention, there reportedly is one of the most remarkable accomplishments in the history of the game that somehow has escaped the attention it deserves.

There is a valuable lesson for all of us who are hooked on golf in the experience realized by one Major James Nesmeth as reported in a book titled *You've Got To Be Believed To Be Heard,* authored by Bert Decker and published by St. Martin's Press.

We pick up the saga of Major Nesmeth's triumph as he was struggling to improve his game. However much he dreamed and struggled, he remained your average weekend golfer, shooting in the mid- to low-90s.

And then for seven long years he did not play, never setting foot on a fairway or indeed touching a club and furthermore suffering deterioration in his physical condition.

The estrangement from the game, however, was involuntary, because Major Nesmeth spent those seven interminable years as a prisoner-of-war in Vietnam.

His imprisonment, moreover, was specially brutal. He was imprisoned in a cage that was approximately four and one-half feet high and five feet long. During almost the entire seven years he saw no one, talked to no one and had virtually no physical activity.

During the first few months he hoped and prayed for his release until he realized that if he did not find some way to occupy his mind he would lose his sanity and probably lose his life.

He decided to take up golf again. From the awful confinement of that tiny prison cell he expanded his mind into thinking about golf, even though he had not played it since leaving for the war.

Each day he would select a golf course and think his way through 18 holes. His thought process took in everything to the last detail. He visualized the clothes he would wear. He conjured up the fragrance of the trees and the freshly-mowed grass. He imagined different weather conditions and played his mental game in all sorts of weather, including sunny summer mornings, windy spring days and tough rainy winter conditions. He thought about the birds and the animals he would encounter on the various courses on which he played his mind game. As he focused with increasing intensity, his imagination came closer and closer to reality.

He could almost feel the grip of the club in his hands. He labored mentally on improving his swing, thinking through the fundamentals and identifying the importance of tempo. In his mind's eye he watched every shot to the point where it landed and then bounced and then rolled and then stopped. He had no place to go, so he was in no hurry. He mentally took every step on his way to the ball and when he got there in his mind, he started working on his next shot. No detail was left out of his mental round. It took him just as long to go around his imaginary course in his mind as it would have if he had been able actually to play a round.

That was his routine, four hours a day, seven days a week for seven very long years.

When he finally was released from that prison cell and arranged to play his first round of golf in seven years, what did he shoot? He shot a smooth 74, that's what he shot—20 strokes better than the golf he had played before his confinement!

To all of us hooked on golf there certainly is a message in this saga. If we can think ourselves into the right frame of mind, if we can focus mentally on what we need to do to execute a proper shot, if we can think our way around a course for 18 holes, we may not be able to duplicate the miracle that Major John Nesmeth was able to develop, but we can enjoyably use our idle moments and we can be better golfers than we ever dreamed possible.

Jack Nicklaus

In any discussion of who was the greatest player in the history of golf, Jack Nicklaus has to emerge with that distinction. His record provides irrefutable proof.

So much has been said and written about him and that record that there is no point in attempting to add to it. Nonetheless, I had an impression from one of his singular performances that I am moved to record.

The performance was his winning the 1993 U.S. Senior Open Championship at Cherry Hills. To put that performance into proper perspective, you have to go back 33 years to the 1960 U.S. Open, also at Cherry Hills.

That 1960 Open brought the fascinating figure of Arnold Palmer into the forefront of the game. It also was yet another Open that Ben Hogan, although well past his prime, almost won. If Ben's third shot on 17 (the 71st hole) had bounced forward toward the hole instead of backward into the water, a lot of golf history might have been different.

In 1960 the Open had the added dimension that was provided by two rounds played on the last day. Hogan was paired with Nicklaus, who was then an amateur, for those last two rounds. Although Nicklaus finished second in that Open, Hogan, after the 4th round, was reported to have said, "If that kid I was paired with had had any brains he would have won by 10 shots!"

That kid developed into the all-time best and there have been few if any players of the game who more effectively applied intellect to the process.

So it was that 33 years later Jack Nicklaus was playing virtually the same golf course on which he had performed so brilliantly in 1960. The compelling point is that in 1993 he was playing the same course with at least as much skill at age 53 as he had demonstrated at age 20 in 1960. I think that performance alone puts Nicklaus' accomplishments into the nonpareil category.

I first saw him play when he dominated the U.S. Amateur Championship in 1961 at Pebble Beach. He was, in a word, awesome. While I marveled at the course-emasculating distances he hit the ball and the moon-shot trajectory of his long irons, the part of his game that impressed me most was the consistency with which he holed putts in the 10-foot range when he needed them. That skill has stayed with him throughout a career in which he must have holed a couple of miles of such putts in crucial situations.

The fortunate fact that a part of Tom Watson's career coincided with a part of Jack's has added a great deal to the history of the game. The duel in the sun at Turnberry in 1977 provided the lore of the game with two of the game's all-time great players playing at the supreme level in the original major championship on a links course. It simply does not get any better than that.

There is more than friendship in their relationship. There is a bond that derives from the reverence for the game that they share. That bond has been a tear producer on occasion. Witness Jack's tearful reaction as he watched Tom play the 72nd hole in the Memorial in 1996 to record Tom's first victory in nine long years. There have been three bear hugs that have brought tears to Tom's eyes; one was at the Memorial, one was at Turnberry and the other at Pebble Beach in 1982.

It was a tonic to observe these two in the twilight of their respective careers team together recently to win a Senior match play championship. Notwithstanding life's vicissitudes with which each of them has had to deal, they still find the skills that made them the giants that they were.

Calvin Peete

A pertinent example of how valuable friendship with Tom Watson has been was the time he partnered me with Calvin Peete.

It was some years ago and Calvin had just begun to emerge as a significant player on the Tour. In a telephone conversation Tom told me that Calvin was one of the more interesting and attractive players who had come along in a long time and asked if I would like to be Calvin's partner in a forthcoming Crosby.

I was delighted at the prospect, but I could not have anticipated all that was in store for me.

I think that Calvin Peete's development as a world-class golfer is one of the more remarkable and inspirational accomplishments in the history of any sport.

As an impoverished African-American youngster he went to work in the vegetable fields in Florida. His observation of the relative affluence of the people who sold used clothing to the field workers led to his getting into that line of business. He distinguished himself from his competition by having a dentist insert a small diamond in one of his upper front teeth. He became known in the trade and among his customers as "the diamond man." That distinction, his salesmanship and effective management of his money provided a stake for investment in some residential rental property so that eventually he became relatively secure financially.

He was in his early twenties when he was first exposed to the game of golf when some friends took him to a public course. To say that he thereupon became hooked on golf is to put it mildly. Dimensions, were added to the game's appeal for him when he learned that people could make a lot of money playing it. He thereupon decided to play his way onto the PGA Tour. For any ordinary person first starting to play at his age, that would have been an impossible dream. The dream becomes pure fantasy when the fact is added that he had an atrophied left arm that he could not straighten, caused by a boyhood accident followed by a botched bone setting.

Calvin Peete, however, was no ordinary person and he set about realizing his fantastic dream with determination which was not to be denied. He read instruction books and taught himself to play. He solved the problem of lack of practice facilities by locating a school yard with some adjacent street lighting where he could practice hitting shots at night.

By his early thirties, his dream had become a reality and he became a significant success story on the PGA Tour.

The year when I played with him in The Crosby, the weather was consistently chilly and windy. Those conditions were unfavorable for him, because his relatively slight frame and his left arm condition limit the strength he could apply to his golf swing. Nonetheless, he played with such resolution and hit the ball so solidly so consistently (he only hit three indifferent golf shots in the whole four rounds) that he finished second (we finished fourth as a team).

We were paired with Tom Watson for three of those rounds. Tom was hitting his drives a long way and consistently outdrove Calvin by 40 to 60 yards. During the last of those three rounds Calvin commented to me about how he dealt with the disadvantage of being a relatively short driver. He said the solution was simple, because all he had to do was to learn to hit the 4 and 5 irons as well as the longer hitters hit their 7 and 8 irons.

What an inspirational role model he should be for all of us and especially for those whose access to the game is complicated by obstacles. I certainly have never been exposed to a more effective example of refusing to allow disadvantage and disability to prevent the realization of a dream. Playing golf with him, especially as his partner in those conditions on the Crosby courses, was pure inspiration.

George Shultz

Among golf's abiding distinctions is the nexus between personal characteristics manifested in playing golf and those apparent in the other aspects of a player's life. A prime example is George Shultz. He plays golf with intensity leavened by a well-developed sense of humor. There is a prevalent element of energetic intelligence applied to the process; he works at getting what he can from his level of skill. He succeeds remarkably, particularly when the situation calls for ability to compete. His attitude and personality contribute to the pleasure of being in his company.

That combination also provided the basis of exemplary career of public service. He served in four cabinet positions for two Presidents. In the Nixon administration, he was Secretary of Labor, Director of the Office of Management and Budget, and Secretary of the Treasury. The culmination of his public career was to serve from 1982 to 1989 in the Reagan administration as Secretary of State. In that role he was the leading architect of the rapprochement with the Soviet Union, which was a prime factor in ending the Cold War and in the demise of the Soviet and Eastern Bloc communism.

His personal characteristics include a self-effacing disposition that, for some observers, may obscure the dimensions of his career. He is in fact one of the more effective and important statesmen of the twentieth century.

Among his many degrees is a B.A. in Economics from Princeton University. That formed the background for a response he gave to a reporter's question about the possibility of his entering the presidential race in 1988. He simply replied that he did not think the American people were ready for a president with a tiger tattooed on his rear end!

In view of his career, his characteristics and his personality, it is both a privilege and a pleasure to be in his company, especially for a round of golf with him.

Rudyard Kipling
and
Pat Ward Thomas

Rudyard Kipling's epic poem titled "IF" includes the lines:

"If you can meet with Triumph and Disaster
and treat those two impostors just the same."

There is a message in those two lines for all of us who are hooked on golf.

Kipling was an English poet, novelist and short-story writer and was one of the literary giants of the Victorian era.

Kipling was an extraordinary golfer.

Arthur Conan Doyle, the creator of Sherlock Holmes, also was a golfer of note and Kipling took golf lessons from him.

In the 1890s Kipling lived for four years in the United States in a country home he built in Vermont.

The extraordinary character of Kipling's golf had at least two features. While he was only 5'6" tall, he hit the ball prodigious distances. Neither the weather nor the lack of a golf course affected Kipling's disposition to play wherever and however he could. He and a fellow lover of the game, a preacher from a nearby Congregational Church, fashioned a course of sorts, playing from the pasture in front of Kipling's house to the Connecticut River two miles away. In the winter they played with red balls on the crust of the snow to tin cans sunk into the snow. When the snow melted the cans were placed in the ground so that the poet/author and the good Reverend could continue to play the game over the rugged Vermont countryside.

That bit of golf history reminds me of another passionate lover of the game whose disposition to play would not be denied simply because there was no course available. He was Pat Ward Thomas, also an English writer who wrote lyrical essays about the game while reporting it in the *Manchester Guardian* and *Country Life*.

Pat fought in the British armed forces in World War II, was captured by the Germans and spent some years in a German prisoner of war compound. Somehow Pat managed while there to turn up a couple of old hickory-shafted golf clubs. He and some other prisoners dug some holes in the ground and did a bit of earth shaping in the exercise yard so as to create a four-hole course. For golf balls they used stones wrapped with adhesive tape. Pat soon had all of the prisoners playing the game on that crude course with those crude implements and probably thereby preserved the sanity of a good many of them.

I played some golf with Pat and otherwise enjoyed the pleasure of his extraordinary company on a number of occasions. His special personality included apparent disdain for, or at least utter indifference with regard to, his attire. His very good friend Alistair Cooke once described his appearance as that of "a Mexican farmer with 100 acres of beans not doing very well."

Pat's journalistic career included covering a golf match in which one of the players played with excruciating deliberation. Pat endured that performance for several holes. Finally, as the perpetrator stood interminably over a putt, Pat loudly proclaimed, "For God's sake, hit it! Can't you see that my life is ebbing away?"

Pat certainly qualified for the distinction of being one of a kind.

The next time any of us has to deal with some less that satisfactory conditioning of a golf course, we could improve our performance by remembering Rudyard Kipling and Pat Ward Thomas and be suitably grateful that we are not playing to tin cans buried in the snow or with golf balls made out of stones covered with adhesive tape.

Tom Watson

Tom's father was an extraordinarily good golfer. He was a graduate student at Stanford University when I was an undergraduate and we played some golf together. When Tom came to Stanford I was naturally interested in him. That interest developed into a friendship that has made a matchless contribution to the experiences I have enjoyed in golf.

In addition to the pleasure of his company, both on and off the golf course, that friendship has enabled me to live vicariously the triumphs and failures of his sensational career.

I also have had the privilege of playing with him in The Crosby and the AT&T at Pebble Beach through all those glorious years when he was the dominant player in the game. That experience provided a proximate vantage point from which to observe all the elements that combined to place him in the pantheon of the game's all time greats.

Those who saw him play in those glory years would recognize those elements as being a near perfect golf swing, verve, heart, intelligence, dogged determination and an intensity of focus that was awesome.

There was flavor to his talent that made watching his play a stimulating experience. He had a wonderfully strong, simple method of propelling the golf ball into what seemed to the ordinary mortal to be the jet stream. One feature of that swing was the arm speed he generated. It was fascinating to watch the arms become a blur.

It was the artistry in his short game, however, that helped moved him from the category of good player to great player. The variety of shots he could play from areas around the green was, to put it mildly, dazzling. Having watched him around the greens use a variety of clubs to cause the ball to react in a variety of ways, I asked him how he had managed to become such a short game virtuoso.

He said that as a little boy it was the part of the game that interested him the most. He expressed that interest with an extraordinary practice regime. He would find a place alongside the practice green posing an almost impossible shot. He would play the shot until, no matter how long it took, he had managed to hole it. He then would find a place with a similar challenge requiring a different kind of shot. The regimen would be repeated until he had exhausted the possibilities and then he would start over. That anecdote says a lot about how he became such a great player.

While the putter became a problem for him as he grew older, in his prime he had to have been among the game's great putters. He seldom hit a putt of any length or combination of breaks without trying to make it and thinking he could. And he did hole them with remarkable frequency. Almost invariably, if he missed, he went by the hole and made it coming back. It was an impressive talent.

His intelligence produced a thoughtfulness in his shot selection that added up to keen course management.

The intelligent approach had other practical uses. For example, in a match play situation when the game was on the line he convinced himself that his opponent was going to execute perfectly. This enabled Tom to concentrate on what he had to do, regardless of what his opponent did, and also took the shock impact out of his opponent doing something spectacular. The best example of that intelligent approach occurred at Turnberry in Scotland in 1977 at the climax of his classic duel with Jack Nicklaus in the British Open. They both were on the last green where Watson had a one shot lead and was $2\frac{1}{2}$ feet from the par-four hole in two shots. Nicklaus was 35 feet away in two needing to make a putt with multiple breaks in it to have any chance. Watson convinced himself that Nicklaus would make that putt, however unlikely, and proceeded simply to concentrate on his $2\frac{1}{2}$-footer. When Jack indeed made the putt, there was no shock effect on Tom who proceeded calmly to roll his putt into the center of the hole to win.

There also was the element of creativity. He could manufacture an astonishing variety of trajectories and directional movements to fit the needs of the shot he had to play.

The crucial element of heart, also known as verve or courage, played a central role in his success. A dramatic example was displayed in that classic duel with Nicklaus at Turnberry. They were on the 71st hole, a short five par. Both had hit excellent tee shots. Watson's second shot was a few yards farther from the green so he played first. He hit a towering three-iron right over the flag stick that finished about 12 feet from the hole. The heart that was on display in that shot took its toll on Jack, who hit an indifferent shot that finished off the green and resulted in Watson taking the one shot lead that was the ultimate margin of his triumph.

A defining element for any great player is a capacity to concentrate that transcends the norm. That capacity separates the great players from the near greats. Tom had it in rare abundance. That capacity translates into an intensity of focus on the shot to be played that mobilizes all of the faculties and eliminates all of the distractions. I once commented to Tom that he could be used to cure cancer, because when he zeroed in on the shot to be played he appeared to be positively radioactive!

The other element that most distinctively identifies the great players is reverence for the game. Tom Watson and the other great players who have so embellished the history of the game manifest a profound depth of feeling for the game, its values, its rules and its traditions.

However distinctive was Tom Watson's golf game and his career, what gave it substance were his character and personality. He has a Huck Finn look that makes him especially attractive and adds to a warm, friendly personality and a lively intelligence. There also is a genuine disposition to have fun.

His career has been embellished by his consummate love affair with the game. That love affair has gone a long way, I believe, to sustain him through the struggle of dealing with nine years and 141 tournaments without a win, 1987–96. His respect for the game which is an integral part of that love affair contributed, I believe, to the dignity with which he dealt with the frustration suffered in those nine long years.

When he revived his game and became again the player he had been by ending that victory drought at the Memorial in 1996, the accomplishment was monumental. More important than that victory was the response he generated among legions of people around the world.

One incident serves to illustrate the abiding nature of his love affair with the game. We were playing in the AT&T at Pebble Beach. His game had reached its nadir when he made a miserable double bogey on the 53rd hole and therefore missed the cut. After that awful round, we had a late lunch at Cypress Point. He looked at his watch as we were leaving the club and said, "It is 4:30; we have time to play nine holes!" So it was that we rounded up shoes and sweaters and borrowed golf clubs from Hank Ketcham (The "Dennis the Menace" creator) and set off to play in the wind and the fog until it was too dark to see. Never has the playing of the game been more pure fun.

Hank Ketcham was involved in another incident which says a good deal about Tom. Tom and I had spent the day working with Robert Trent Jones Jr. on the design of The Links At Spanish Bay. Hank joined us for dinner at the Pebble Beach Lodge. A good deal of wine contributed to the convivial atmosphere. Near the end of the meal, Tom disappeared and returned in golf attire clutching his sand wedge and some golf balls. He said, "Come on, let's go play the shot!" (He was referring to the shot he had holed on 17 when he won the U.S. Open.)

It was about 11 o'clock on a pitch black, moonless night when the four of us managed to locate the 17th green. There ensued a spirited discussion of four different views of the place from which the shot had been struck and where the hole had been located. The one view that seemed to carry the least weight was Watson's. Eventually a consensus was reached and a couple of dozen assorted efforts were made to reproduce "the shot." It is fortuitous that the results were not recorded.

Among the other highlights for me of my relationship with him was a trip we took to play golf in Ireland and Scotland on his way to play in the 1981 British Open. My recollections of that trip were recorded in a piece I wrote published in *Golf Digest* as follows:

Irish Whisky, Scottish Gorse,
Tom Watson and Me

By Frank D. Tatum Jr. (*Golf Digest*, July 1982)

Tom Watson and I were on the third hole at Dornoch in Scotland. The weather was wet and blustery, giving those glorious links just the right combination of challenges. With the wind whipping his clothing and the rain spattering his face, Tom turned to me with a look of absolute joy and said, "This is the most fun I've had playing golf in my whole life."

That comment was the culmination of an odyssey that began with a telephone call from Tom. How would any golfer feel about answering the telephone, finding Tom Watson on the line and hearing him say, "Let's take a trip the week before the British Open and play golf in Ireland and Scotland." My reaction was to wonder how I could handle the anticipation while working through the months between Watson's call and that week.

Tom and I have been good friends for a number of years. I was a contemporary of his father at Stanford University (by no coincidence, Ray Watson was a very good player). Our friendship developed during Tom's years at Stanford. We maintained contact after he graduated and started playing the tour. I've had the privilege of playing as Tom's partner in several Bing Crosby Pro-Ams, and it's been fascinating to watch his development through the window of that tournament.

Despite his record in the British Open, I have kidded Watson that he didn't know anything about British seaside golf. I once told the then three-time British Open champion that I would gladly give him a series of playing lessons there if he were ever interested.

Arranging the details for accommodations and play in the months preceding the trip, I realized that what lay before me was *the ultimate golf vacation*. Imagine the dual pleasure of Tom Watson's company, on the one hand, and of British and Irish golf, on the other.

The week preceding our trip had been enervating for Tom. He had suffered through some bad golf at Butler National in the Western Open, worked in Kansas City on Monday, returned to Chicago that night where he entertained a business group at dinner and then played golf with them on the following day at Medinah. My wife Barbara and I met Tom and his wife Linda at the airport in New York that Tuesday evening. When we got on the plane, Tom seemed to be very tired—an impression that was confirmed when he said, "Before we play golf tomorrow, let's get a couple of hours sleep at the hotel." He had almost no sleep on the 5½-hour flight to Shannon where we arrived at 7 a.m. local time.

The spectacle that was southwest Ireland and the thought of playing Ballybunion apparently revived him, however, because there was no mention of going to the hotel for some sleep; rather he suggested that we stop only long enough to change clothes and get to the course as soon as possible.

We took a route that included an auto ferry trip across the Shannon River. There were several other cars on the ferry. We soon learned that every one of them was full of people on the way to Ballybunion to watch Watson play golf. One carload had come all the way from a suburb of Belfast in Northern Ireland. They had been on the road for six hours, having left their home at 3 a.m.

I had tried to keep his plans as private as possible, because a basic purpose of the trip was to give him the opportunity to play courses in Ireland and Scotland as a private golfer rather than a public performer. An Irishman, observing the 1,000 or so people who turned up at Ballybunion, later said: "You made a mistake trying to keep it a secret. There is no way anyone can keep a secret in Ireland. You should have published it in the newspapers and then nobody would have believed it!"

The Arrival at Ballybunion

As we turned into the private drive leading to the Ballybunion Golf Club, I noticed a large American flag flying from the club's flagpole. As the car moved up the hill toward the clubhouse, the hundreds who had been waiting all morning burst into applause. It was the first of a continuing sequence of expressions of warm feelings for

84

him, both as a person and as a player.

As the crowd pressed in around us on the first tee trying to get as close to him as possible, I worried about how many would get in the way of one of the errant shots I undoubtedly was going to hit. As the fates would have it, all of them escaped unharmed.

As Tom responded to the feel and the flavor of those God-given links and to the ebullient enthusiasm of the crowd, any vestige of weariness dissolved. He took one quick practice swing, and, with the driver practically scraping noses on the backswing, he hit an absolutely marvelous tee shot well clear of the cemetery that haunts the visage of that first shot. I supposed his approach to the 72nd green at Turnberry at the British Open in 1977 elicited a louder crowd response, but I cannot believe that any shot he has ever hit anywhere has been greeted with more enthusiastic appreciation.

The Game Was On!

It was a lovely day with only scattered clouds and a mild breeze. Harry Easterly, the senior executive director of the USGA, was vacationing in Ireland with his wife Mary, and he played with us.

Ballybunion and Watson were a perfect match. He was effusive in his praise of the course. He commented on the marvelous variety of challenges presented on almost every tee, on how most of the holes are only fully visible after you reach your tee shot so that the distinctive demands of each shot are presented sequentially rather than all at once, giving each its maximum impact, on how sensational are the remaining requirements of the shots into the greens and on how spectacularly the course fits into the massive dunes that make up its terrain.

Watson Has a 72

He played it wonderfully well, particularly considering his lack of sleep. The greens were not quite up to Ballybunion standards; uncharacteristically, he did not hole anything of consequence. He scored 72, evoking all sorts of expressions of appreciation from the crowd as he hit one beautiful shot after another.

As we approached the 14th green I heard the club secretary say to Tom, "We have a bit of drink for you here." The comment puzzled me, because facilities for drinking are virtually nonexistent on golf courses in Ireland. I need not have puzzled, because when we reached the green I saw a small table set up alongside it covered with Irish linen on which there were some glasses and two very large bottles of Irish whisky. "A bit of drink" looked like enough to fuel a very large wake! After we putted out, the president of the club, the club captain, the ladies captain, the secretary and we each were poured what can only be described as a considerable slug of Irish whisky. It was 8 a.m. New York time and a slug of Irish whisky was not exactly in our frame of reference. It went down very smoothly, however, with instant warming effect.

As dozens of cameras promptly appeared, recording the scene, the charming lady captain, who is the mother of six, said to me, "Oh, my goodness, hide me, please. My mother does not know I drink!"

That bit of imbibing having been accomplished, we repaired to the 15th tee where we looked at one of the best par-three holes that exists anywhere in the world. Tom, emboldened with Irish whisky beginning to work on him, said, "How far is it, Tatum"

I replied, "It is 228 yards, Watson."

He said, "Watch me blister a 1-iron."

Blister a 1-iron he did with a shot that had all of the majesty of that majestic hole. If there was anyone in that crowd who had not yet reached the adulation stage, that shot in that setting did it.

A Return to Ballybunion

The whole flavor of the occasion was such that I was moved to wish the round would never end. The wish partially was granted when, near the end of the round, Tom, in a remarkable reversal of his approach to the day expressed in New York, quietly said to me, "Do you think, after the gallery has gone home, that we could arrange to play some more?" We certainly could.

When we finished the round we discovered that our Irish hosts had arranged another ceremony. A table had been set up next to the flagpole from which the small club flag and large American flag were standing in the breeze. In appreciation of Tom's play and of his coming to Ballybunion, the club officials presented the Watsons with a piece of Waterford crystal.

We then were treated to an elaborate meal for which the word "lunch" is not remotely adequate. Thereupon we went back to the hotel, slept for an hour and were picked up there by the club secretary who drove us back to the sixth tee where, shortly after 7 p.m., we set out for 13 more holes. The coloring of Ballybunion in the summer twilight with the huge dunes casting surreal shadows is perfectly beautiful. Tom's hopes for getting around unnoticed lasted about two holes. People playing the course spotted him, stopped playing and soon formed a small gallery. That gallery attracted others from the clubhouse and its environs so that before we had played five holes we were accompanied by 100-plus people.

The club somehow discovered that it was Tom's and Linda's eighth wedding anniversary. Copious quantities of champagne provided the liquid premises for a suitable celebration so that the first day of the odyssey ended as buoyantly as it had begun.

Portmarnock Is Next

On Thursday morning we flew to Dublin and drove directly from the airport to Portmarnock, where we were warmly greeted by a contingent of club dignitaries. A light lunch reinforced with Irish beer was flavored by the presence of Harry Bradshaw. Harry, the resident pro at Portmarnock, was a significant factor in British and Irish golf before the war. His place in the history of the game was secured when his tee shot on the fifth hole at Royal St. George's in the 1949 British Open came to rest in the bottom half of a broken bottle. Harry played it from there, simply by whacking the bottle with a full swing, instead of taking relief, a decision that turned out to be critical when Harry tied Bobby Locke for the championship and lost in a playoff.

Several hundred people were with us as we thoroughly enjoyed playing Portmarnock. The gallery included a number of reporters. One of them had called the club secretary to confirm that Tom was scheduled to play. When the secretary protested that Tom was hoping to enjoy a private round of golf, the reporter responded, "After he won his second Open championship, he lost his right to privacy."

On to Prestwick

After a characteristically convivial bit of drink in the clubhouse, we returned to the airport, flew to Glasgow and went on to the Marine Hotel at Troon. Early the next morning we were on the first tee at Prestwick, trying to identify the landing area (there's nothing to see except a stone wall marking out-of-bounds on the right and sand hills covered with gorse and whin bushes, behind which you later discover the fairway is hidden).

I knew Tom would enjoy it, because Prestwick is such a delightful museum piece. He did more than enjoy it; he reveled in it. The blind shots amused him, the humps and hillocks challenged him and the timber-reinforced bunkers impressed him.

We had a Nassau bet on each of our rounds together. He gave me strokes, of course. The stakes were modest by any standard and most certainly in relation to the prize money that is his usual stake in the game. Nonetheless, he competed with an amused intensity that added a lot to the fun of playing with him. Every shot he planned and executed with meticulous care. I do not think he ever in any circumstance plays a careless shot. He kept track of our games so that it seemed to matter a lot, and in all sorts of ways he expressed real interest in how and where I was hitting the ball.

His sense of humor, which is well developed, has a pixie quality. He never missed an opportunity to tweak me in an amusing way. For example, when we reached the 18th tee at Prestwick, the gallery that had assembled from heaven knows where pressed in around the very small tee. He had closed me out on the 18-hole portion of our match, but we were all square on the back nine. I had the honor; as

I teed up my ball he said to me with a little grin, "Aren't you going to press me?" The last hole is 295 yards long, structured so that he is likely to drive the green. Nonetheless, my pride would not permit refusal of such a public challenge, so I replied, "Given the odds that I will play this hole better than you will, I could hardly pass up such an offer; I accept." Whereupon I hooked a drive into the deep rough and he hit his pin high just off the green.

As I made the desultory walk into the rough, he followed right behind me, made a rather meticulous inspection of the lie of my ball and stood nearby while I played the shot.

My caddie, with that heavy Scottish brogue that poses such a language barrier on the links, said, "Wah' are ya doin' over here, Mr. Watson, are ya thinkin' he might be improvin' his lie?" As a fitting footnote to that triumph of repartee, I holed my putt for the birdie to halve the hole.

After lunch, we played Troon before a large gallery. Tom played brilliantly producing seven birdies in the first eleven holes on a very demanding golf course.

After the round, the captain invited us into the clubhouse where, as it developed, he had arranged a celebration, having somehow discovered that it was my birthday. A toast with champagne moved me to respond with an inadequate, but nonetheless heartfelt, expression of what it meant to be able to celebrate my birthday playing golf with Tom Watson at Prestwick and Troon and to be feted in such company in the Troon clubhouse.

On the following morning, we flew from Glasgow to Inverness and then drove for two pleasant hours, along Scotland's northeastern coastline to Dornoch. There we encountered our first and only day of typical British links weather; that is, it was blowing about 20 knots with fairly heavy rain squalls. It clearly pleased Tom; he liked the added challenge inclement weather brought to the game.

We started off at 1:30 p.m. followed by several hundred people, many of whom had come long distances to see him play. Dornoch has often been identified as the quintessential links course. Judging from the obvious pleasure with which he played it, I think Tom would agree.

He dealt with the course and the conditions brilliantly, going out in 36 and coming home in 32. As we walked up the 18th fairway, he quietly asked me whether I thought we could get out again that evening by ourselves. I arranged to have the caddies put the clubs away and go on home. Tom and I relaxed in the clubhouse until all of the gallery had gone home. The caddies came back and at about 6:30 p.m., with the wind a bit stronger and the rain a bit heavier, off we went for another round. At that hour and in those conditions we did manage to get all the way around by ourselves. It was in that setting that Tom remarked about this being the most fun he had ever had playing golf.

Sandy Wins a Round

By no means incidentally, this was the one round on the trip in which I managed to beat him with the strokes he was giving me. We finished the first nine all even and carried the bets over. As we walked off the 15th green where I had holed a birdie putt to go 2 up on him, he said, "I will press." I accepted with an appropriate expression of gratitude.

When we reached the 16th tee, however, and he recalled the hole and the fact that I had a stroke on it, he said, "I won't press." I told him that it had to be one of my unluckier moments of my whole life, because here was Tom Watson, seriously trying to back out of a press bet that he had made with me and I only had two witnesses (our caddies), both of whom lived at least 6,000 miles from the places where I would be recounting this incredible story to disbelieving audiences.

I then gave him a little lecture on the law of offer and acceptance and the ethical questions involved in attempting to renege. The salutary effect of all that was dramatically illustrated when he hooked his tee shot into an awful place in a quarry that borders the left side of the 16th fairway. The triumph was thereby secured.

We finished the round at about 9 p.m., wet, windblown, weary, but warmly glowing with the fulfillment of a golfing experience that was perfectly beautiful.

At one of our more serious moments, I remember talking with Watson about a deeply disturbing trend among the links of the British Isles. Automated watering systems are being used with other stimulants for growing grass so that these courses are acquiring the lush, cemetery-green look and the inevitable consequence of that look—soft, slow greens. The distinctive character of links golf—the bounce of the ball and the shotmaking requirements that go with it—is being lost. The need to calculate for a good deal of bounce and roll in the shot makes the links game a much more interesting, exciting and demanding game than that played almost entirely in the air. These are Tom's views and he felt them so strongly that he was moved to express them at a press conference the next week at the British Open at Royal St. George's. He put it as accurately and as diplomatically as he could by saying that he regretted the Americanization of British courses.

Vacation Drawing to an End

At 8:30 the last morning of our vacation Tom and I and several hundred Scots were on the first tee at Dornoch. As we walked along the first fairway Tom said to me, "Don't you ever get tired?"

I replied, "I certainly do, but put me vertical and give me the feel of seaside turf through my spikes and I could go on forever."

When we reached the green, Tom looked around at the array of people surrounding the green and said, "Doesn't anyone in Scotland go to church?" He later observed, as the gallery filled out, that most of the additions were women, indicating that the churches in the area that morning had been largely populated by women.

There was something indescribably special about that gallery. They were golfers with a manifest appreciation for the game. The pleasure they derived from watching Tom play was compelling. As the feeling for what they were witnessing continued to build, Tom responded with a virtuoso performance that was literally moving to watch.

As we moved into the final holes of that last round at Dornoch, I slowed my pace, because of the very strong sense of not wanting the trip to end. I stretched the last few holes of it for as long as I could.

A Treat for the Caddie

Arranging to get Tom and Linda to the house near Royal St. George's where they were to stay during the British Open required a helicopter ride over the highlands to Edinburgh. That flight, skimming the ridges of that somberly beautiful part of Scotland, was a fitting capper to the trip.

A suitable footnote also was provided by the caddie I had enjoyed at Dornoch. He was a handsome young man, a member of the club, obviously a good golfer with deep feelings about the game. During those three rounds at Dornoch we had developed a very warm rapport. As I shook his hand before climbing into the helicopter, I said, "Thanks for adding so much to a memorable weekend. A special part of it for me was the sense I had of your enjoyment in watching someone who can really play, hit the variety of wonderful golf shots you saw and engineer this golf course in such a masterful fashion."

With a delighted twinkle in his eye he replied, "Yes, and Tom Watson wasn't bad, either."

Among his distinctive features is the depth of his roots. He has never left Kansas where he was born. It is part of the Watson lore that, while his elitist peers were buying boats and moving to Florida, he was hitting shots in the winter from a mat through an open barn door out into the snow.

The money Tom has raised for Stanford University says a lot about him. That activity evolved out of a conversation I had with him responding to his question about how he could be useful to Stanford. We arranged a series of "outings" modeled on the corporate outings that have added so much to the wealth of successful golfers. Potential donors were invited to a day with Tom (who contributed his time and effort) that started with a short game clinic, proceeding with a game of golf organized so that he played a few holes with each four-ball. Lunch was followed by seminars with some of Stanford's faculty superstars and then dinner with the president of the University. People who attended those outings in the aggregate have contributed more than $100,000,000 to Stanford!

Tom has strong convictions and he has the courage of those convictions, even when it has cost him some adverse publicity. When he thought Bill Murray had crossed the line of sensible behavior whirling an elderly woman into a bunker at "The AT&T," he said so and took some flak from some media and other types. When a Jewish applicant for membership in the Kansas City Country Club was turned down apparently because of his religion, Tom resigned a membership he had enjoyed since he was a little boy. When Gary McCord violated precepts of good taste and judgment on a Masters telecast, Tom wrote private letters to the telecast's producer and to the president of the club expressing his views of that performance.

It says an awful lot about the taste and judgment of many in the media that Tom was roundly criticized for having expressed himself about McCord's performance. He also received a distressing lot of abuse in the mail disagreeing with Tom's views of that matter. If so-called journalists and other people think that references to pubic hair and body bags are appropriate on a Masters telecast, it is their taste and judgment that ought to be questioned, not Tom's.

In the 1994 AT&T his golf game had revived to the point where he was positioned to win it after the third round. My play as his partner in the pro-am competition, however, had been so mediocre that when we finished the third round we thought we had missed the cut as a team. There was, of course, a good deal of interest in his revival so that after that third round he was the feature attraction in the press tent. As he emerged from a press conference that had focused on whether Watson indeed was back, his wife Linda was waiting for him and asked how he felt about it. His response was, "We made the cut!" To have been thinking about us rather than himself in that setting tells you a lot about the sort of person he is.

Perhaps the most expressive way for me to sum him up as I see him is to quote a toast I gave at a ceremony at Stanford University honoring him:

"If you play the game for all that it is worth

If you measure its worth in values that transcend money

If your object in performance is simply to be the best
you can be

If your life long love affair with the game has done a lot
for the lives of others as well as for yours

If your qualities include adding considerably to the
pleasure of others with whom you play

If the integrity of your golf swing is a reflection of the
integrity of your character

Then who you are in essence is Tom Watson

And it is to that essence Tom Watson that we are here
gathered to raise our glasses in a toast."

Opportunities Lost as Tiger Woods Goes for Gold

As I think about the mind-boggling amounts of money being paid to professional athletes, I am reminded of the response that Babe Ruth is reported to have given when asked how he felt about being paid more than the President of the United States. Babe's reported response was, "I had a better year than he did!" Nonetheless, it is difficult to rationalize how much athletes are being paid these days to play games. There is a distressing fallout from that phenomenon evident in the numbers of young men, and now women, who are sacrificing opportunities to develop as mature, educated people to the illusion that all they need to do to succeed in life is develop their athletic skills.

When Tiger Woods elected to go to Stanford University, he expressed himself to the effect that maturing and becoming educated had priority in his life over becoming a professional golfer. I was encouraged, not just for Tiger, but for all the young people, particularly black young people, who could be influenced by his example. As he continued to develop as a student and a golfer at Stanford that encouragement took on additional dimensions. It was in that context that I watched on television one of the most gut-gripping events I have ever witnessed—the final match of the 1996 United States Amateur Championship. Tiger's triumph in that final so as to earn the distinction of winning three consecutive U.S. Amateur Championships obviously was going to increase the pressure on him to leave Stanford and become a professional golfer.

On the day after that final match, therefore, I was moved to write him the following letter:

August 26, 1996
Tiger Woods

Dear Tiger:

I do not presume that you need, or would even be interested in, this letter. I write nonetheless, because I think that the opportunity that you have is not just unique, but monumentally important.

I should identify the fact that you and I are the sole members of an exclusive group; that is, you and I are the only two players in the extraordinary history of Stanford golf to have won the individual NCAA Championship! To say that you have added ultimate luster to that group is a gross understatement.

As I see it, the opportunity you have is on two levels. One is the personal level. There you have the opportunity to use Stanford to provide you with the education that you need to give your life real substance. It is worth noting here that you can anticipate at least another 60 years of occupancy on this planet and the effectiveness of every one of those 60 years is going to be critically affected by how intellectually equipped and mature you are when you take on the real world. You are not going to develop that equipment playing professional golf.

Staying at Stanford as an amateur also would provide the opportunity to develop your potential as a player freed from the cauldron of professional golf. There are some examples of how useful this opportunity can be, most recently that of the experience of Gordon Sherry.

The utility of the foregoing opportunities is considerably enhanced by the insulation provided by your continuing to be an amateur and a student at Stanford. While the pressure and attention will continue to be intense, the insulation that Stanford provides will add immeasurably to your ability to deal with it so as not to be distracted from what should be your ultimate goals.

Obviously those goals have to include your becoming an

educated person. When he was president of Stanford, Wally Sterling defined an educated person as someone who can entertain himself, a friend and an idea!

The other level of your opportunity is to make a statement that could matter more than anything else you ever do. That statement can be made both by what you do and by what you say about it. The statement simply is that there is infinitely more to be had in and from a life than making barrels full of money and having extravagant public exposure. If money and exposure are all someone has, then in essence he has less than nothing (there are some awful examples provided by athletes, that illustrate this point). The essential measure of a life is what you do with it throughout its whole span for yourself, for your friends and for your community. The essence of the statement, therefore, is that there is no price that can be put on the opportunity to develop fully as a mature and as an educated person.

That statement takes on particular resonance because of your ethnic background. Coming from a Caucasian it would not get much attention. Coming from someone with your background, and especially from someone who has made such a spectacular impression you have so far managed to make, could matter beyond any measure that I can think of. That measure has to include the awful tragedy of so many young people, particularly black young people, sacrificing their development as whole human beings to the illusion that they can have a satisfactory life simply by developing their athletic skills.

As I see it, Tiger, in terms of attracting people to the game of golf you have more potential than anyone who has come along at least since Bobby Jones. Considerably beyond that in importance is the fact that a combination of circumstances has positioned you to have considerably more influence on the broader community than Jones could ever have dreamed of. If you cease to be an amateur golfer and turn professional before finishing your education at Stanford, those two potentials are considerably diminished.

Obviously you have extraordinary, perhaps unique, potential for playing professional golf. The issue is not whether, but when you take on that career. There is no reason to believe that that potential, both in money value and performance, will not increase as you continue to mature and develop at Stanford. There is every reason to believe that your influence on the game and the community would increase exponentially.

I trust the foregoing manifests how fervently I hope you make the right decision. In any event, it is expressed with every good wish for you and your future.

Sincerely,

Sandy Tatum

The letter was not sent, because the word was passed that he was turning pro before it was mailed. I have no illusions that, if it had reached him at a time when he could have considered it, it would have affected his decision. Nonetheless, I think a matchless opportunity was lost and I continue to wish that he had not lost it.

That continuing wish led me later to write an open letter to him which *Sports Illustrated* published:

Dear Tiger:

You and I share the privilege of having attended Stanford and the distinction of being the only students from the university to win the NCAA golf title. Given the commonality of our experiences, I feel that I'm in a position to offer you some advice, and I hope you'll take it as seriously as it is given. My advice: Finish your education at Stanford.

For one thing, doing so would fulfill the promise you made to your parents in August 1996 when you turned pro. Attending classes would also afford you a respite from the pressure cooker into which your success has cast you. Such a respite would not only give you the opportunity to lead something resembling a normal life but might also extend your time as golf's preeminent player. Pundits postulate that the primary threat to your career is back trouble. I think you run a greater risk of burning out. If I were you, I'd use the fall quarters at Stanford—when the Tour season slows considerably—to complete my education.

There is, however, another motive for my advice. You have an opportunity to make a statement to the deluded young people who think that superior athletic ability is all that's needed to live a fulfilling life. They ignore the fact that an insignificant percentage of athletes succeed on the professional level, and of those who do, many are left unfulfilled once their careers are over. By becoming a millionaire almost overnight, you have only added to the siren call heard by so many young athletes.

I offer two role models for you. The first is Chad Hutchinson, the standout Stanford pitcher and quarterback who was offered $1.5 million to sign with the Atlanta Braves after his senior year of high school in 1995. Although his mother, Martha, was struggling to raise a large family, Chad turned down the offer. When Martha was asked about her son's decision, she wanted to know how anyone could trade an education for money.

The other example is Bobby Jones. Before he retired from competitive golf at 28, he had won 13 major championships and established himself as the game's greatest player while earning a degree in mechanical engineering from Georgia Tech, a degree in English literature from Harvard and passing the Georgia bar exam. What Jones did had a profound influence on thousands of young people, including me.

Even Jones, though, didn't have the same opportunity to affect the lives of young people as you do.

      Sincerely,

      Frank (Sandy) Tatum Jr.

I do not discount how alluring was the offer to become suddenly wildly rich and to get started on his quest for his Grail. Obviously, more than money motivates Tiger. His superhuman focus is on being the best, not just of his time, but of all time. While this is an increasingly realistic objective, his career could have transcendent import and impact if he were to use his influence as I have suggested.

The
Governance
of the
Game

The Royal and Ancient Golf Club of St. Andrews

The development of the game of golf with its values intact is the product of proper governance of the game free of conflicts of interest and commercial objectives. The game was originated by amateur golfers and it is they who make up the overwhelming majority (99-plus percent) of those who play it. While professional golfers have contributed profoundly to the development of the game, their numbers in relation to the many millions of amateurs are statistically insignificant.

It is eminently sensible, therefore, that the game should be governed by amateurs.

The origins of that governance go back to the development of a private golf club in the Kingdom of Fife in Scotland.

There is something supernatural in the history and development of the role of the Royal and Ancient Golf Club of St. Andrews (the "R&A") in the evolution of the game of golf. That thought has several elements.

The most impressive is that this private golf club located in a relatively remote area of the northeast coast of Scotland evolved as the governing body of golf wherever it is played on the planet excepting only in the United States and Mexico. The United States and Mexico, moreover, essentially adopted the basic elements of the leadership of the R&A.

The evolution got its impetus in the 18th century as golf and golf clubs began to proliferate in Scotland. Since the game then had no governing body, each club was inclined to set its own rules to define the game being played there. Somehow those individual clubs came to independent conclusions that each should adopt and play by the rules which had been developed by the R&A for play on the Old Course and further concluded to continue to play by such rules as the R&A continued to evolve, refine and interpret them. It is these rules, so interpreted, that essentially define the game of golf.

In view of the disposition of human beings for independence, and understanding that the R&A had and has no means to impose its will, I think these developments qualify as being supernatural.

Obviously, these developments could not have occurred if the R&A had not established a pervading impression of rock-solid integrity and purity of approach to preserving the traditions and values of a developing game.

There are two other elements in this supernatural picture.

One is the Old Course. How can the development of this masterpiece be explained except in metaphysical terms? Alistair Cooke puts this element into proper perspective in an introduction he wrote to a Sir Guy Campbell book on the game's history:

"Sir Guy Campbell's classic account of the formation of the links beginning with Genesis and moving step-by-step to the thrilling arrival of "tilth" on the fingers of coastal land, suggest that such notable features of our planet as dinosaurs, the prairies, the Himalayas, the seagull, the female of the species herself, were accidental byproducts of the Almighty's preoccupation with the creation of The Old Course at St. Andrews."

There also is the R&A clubhouse. It so perfectly expresses the image of the qualities and characteristics that so distinguish the R&A, that mere mortals must have had some other worldly help in designing it.

To those of us who find in the game experiences and emotions in some respects that transcend those realized in the rest of our lives, it follows rather logically that the aura of the R&A should have a supernatural flavor.

The United States
Golf Association

The R&A played a critical role in the origins of the United States Golf Association ("USGA"). A prime mover in the origins was Charles Blair Macdonald, who probably did more than any other single individual to establish the game in the United States.

Fortunately, he was for a time a student at the University of St. Andrews, where he was introduced to the game, to the part that the R&A was playing in its development and to the Old Course. He also was the beneficiary of lessons given him by Old Tom Morris.

That exposure resulted in his manifold contributions to the development of golf in this country, including designing the first 18-hole golf course on this side of the Atlantic and a number of other notable courses. His most important contribution, however, was to have been a prime mover in the creation of the USGA in New York in December of 1894.

The USGA has ever since been the governing body of golf in this country. It adopted the rules promulgated by the R&A and followed the precedent of having amateur golfers as the governors of the game.

As the game evolved in the first half of this century, the spirit of 1776 turned up in the USGA and some differences developed in the rules decreed by the respective governing bodies. The developing dichotomy was terminated in 1952 when, in a monumental diplomatic triumph, the two governing bodies agreed on a uniform set of rules applicable worldwide.

While the role and the influence of the R&A has been virtually universal, the import and impact of the USGA certainly needs to be recognized. Obviously, the development of golf in the United States, including the numbers of its citizens who are enshrined in golf's pantheon, has given the game monumental impetus.

The game exists only because there are rules that define it and a governing authority to develop and interpret those rules. These principles were given a severe jolt recently when Ely Callaway persuaded Arnold Palmer to help Ely merchandise an illegal club. That startling development provoked me to write the following letter to Arnold:

Mr. Arnold Palmer   *October 31, 2000*
Bay Hill Club
900 Bay Hill Boulevard
Orlando, Florida 32811

Dear Arnold:

My first reaction was disbelief, i.e. that the report was dead wrong. I then thought that you must have been misquoted. I may be missing something, Arnold. If so, I would be relieved to learn what it is. Absent such revelation, however, the following is my reaction to what somehow you have been persuaded to do and say.

Apparently Ely Callaway perceives a marketing opportunity in clubs which do not conform to the Rules of Golf. While that is Ely's prerogative, it strikes me as akin to marketing balls (aka "hot balls") which do not conform and are sold as going much farther than those that do. It is, of course, your prerogative to give Ely's marketing project the credibility that you specially can give it. What I cannot understand, however, is how you, perhaps the most respected, indeed revered, figure in the whole history of the game of golf, could consent to help merchandise a non-conforming club.

A game can only be identified by the rules that define it. The game of golf is defined by the Rules of Golf. A premise for what you and Ely are doing, as I understand it, is that the only people who need the game of golf are professional golfers. The rest of us 25,000,000 golfers, therefore, are left with a choice to play an undefinable game which has no rules.

What happens, in that case, to our handicap system, our $2 Nassaus, our monthly medals, our club championships and our city, state and national championships?

People playing with hot clubs and/or hot balls may have fun, but they are not playing an identifiable defined game. It may qualify as fun to pay megabucks for a club that acts like a slingshot on the ball. As I see it, however, the real fun derives from dealing with the challenges that makes the game of golf so enduringly fascinating.

The road on which you have embarked with Ely, Arnold, is one which replaces the game of golf with what in real effect is a non game without rules to identify and define it. That road leads away from a fundamental premise that golf is a definable game and it is, or at least should be, the only game that everyone, professional or amateur, plays whenever and wherever he or she tees it up.

I simply cannot understand how you could have been persuaded to take that road.

Sincerely,
Frank (Sandy) Tatum, Jr.

My experience with the USGA as a member of the Executive Committee and as its President was an education in how complex the governance of the game in this country has become and how much it matters to have that governance provided by amateur golfers whose only stake is their love of the game.

The Rules of Golf
and Some Rulings

Defining the Game

The rules of golf get mixed reviews from those who play the game. For some, they are the game's bible and they are accorded commensurate respect. For others, they are the game's Internal Revenue Code and they are much maligned as being ridiculously complex and beyond the understanding of ordinary mortals. I am moved to say that these dissidents are guilty of laying a bum rap on the rules and those who make them.

In considering what and who is right, we should start with the fundamental premise that it is the rules that define the game we are playing. When you and I tee up on the first tee and say we are going to play golf, the rules define what we mean and, most importantly, assure that we are both playing the same game. We can, of course, make up our own rules, but if we do, we are not going to be playing golf and we will not be playing the same game as others on the course who are playing golf.

The anarchy that developed from separate groups of players making up their own rules led to the extraordinary, indeed virtually miraculous, evolution of the Rules of Golf. That evolution is one of the more stimulating sagas of individuals intelligently giving up their individual preferences for the sake of uniformity.

Critics of the Rules complain that there are too many of them and that they are too complex. The problem is that golf provides a virtually infinite variety of situations, which the rules must accommodate. For example, how do the rules deal with a ball coming to rest alongside a coiled rattlesnake? Is the player confronted with the lousy choice of putting his life on the line or taking a stroke and distance penalty? For some people hooked on golf such a choice would pose a very close call. It is comforting to note that the rules, however, accommodate that dilemma in a much more equitable way.

There are few, if any, areas of human endeavor where nearly as many millions of man and woman hours have been so devoted to a cause; the cause, that is, of continuing to develop rules that are sensible and understandable. Those men and women are the unsung heroes of the game and they deserve our profound gratitude.

We also should be grateful for the critically important distinction that golf enjoys, that is, that all players of the game, professional and amateur, have consented to be governed by ruling bodies made up of amateur golfers with no stake in their governance, excepting only their abiding love of the game they are governing.

Respect for the Rules

Among golf's many distinctions is respect for the rules, which is the fundamental premise for the playing of the game. That premise certainly distinguishes it from football, which requires several officials scrutinizing every play for rules infractions and where the prevalent players' attitude is to get away with whatever they can. In baseball, pitchers' careers have been based on getting away with the spitter. The game of tennis has become afflicted with gross, at times bizarre, disputes over whether balls have landed in or out.

As a dramatic contrast illustrating the spirit in which golf is played, there is a celebrated incident involving Bobby Jones. At a critical point in a match, Jones hooked his tee shot into some woods. No one but Jones and his caddie saw what then occurred. When he emerged from the woods, having played back into the fairway, Jones announced that he had incurred a penalty stroke, because his ball had moved after he had addressed it. To have so acted was not unusual, because the prevalent attitude of golfers is to play by the rules. What makes the incident so distinctive, however, was Jones' response when commended for what he had done. He said simply, "You might as well commend someone for not robbing a bank!"

To qualify for identification as a golfer requires respect, if not reverence, for the rules of the game. The vast majority of people who play do so qualify. Golf is universally played without whistle blowing officials assuring compliance with the rules. In golf, the pervading credo is to blow the whistle on yourself. That this elementary characteristic identifies golf as being distinctive in a way is a sad commentary on so many other sports which do not have it.

The Spring-Effect Dilemma

Recently, two developments have violated the premise that there be a singular game of golf played everywhere in the world. One was the decision of the R&A to have no standard to define spring-like effect in a golf club. The other was the decision by Callaway to market clubs in the United States that did not conform to the standards established by the USGA. Those developments, singularly and much more collectively, are seriously divisive.

These developments occurred with reference to a single Rule of Golf, i.e., an identical rule specified in the rules published by the R&A and the USGA respectively. The rule in both rule books provides in pertinent part:

"The material and construction of the clubhead shall not have the effect at impact of a spring…"

That rule has been in both the R&A and USGA rule books since 1984. The rule was developed in response to a manufacturer that claimed to have created a "flex iron," i.e., a club with a clubhead designed to give the ball a slingshot effect. The rule reflected a principle that a slingshot effect was not an appropriate part of the production of a golf shot.

The "flex iron," therefore, was outlawed and became a historic artifact. Focus on the rule reoccurred when titanium faces on oversized clubheads added a slingshot effect to the contact with the ball. It became necessary, therefore, to establish a standard which would identify what constitutes spring-like effect. The USGA did so with a test identified as "COR" which uses coefficient of restitution to establish a limit on clubhead design that can produce a slingshot effect.

Callaway apparently perceived a market in the United States and Canada for clubs which violated the rule so developed and, using Arnold Palmer as its prime marketing vehicle, launched a campaign to sell so called ERC II drivers in the United States.

Analysis of this development requires understanding of two basic premises:

- an organized game requires a set of rules to define it; and
- there has to be a governing authority to establish and interpret those rules

When I use the term the game of golf I refer to the game identified in the Rules of Golf published and administered by the USGA. In my view, therefore, playing with the ERC II is not playing golf, but rather is playing an unidentifiable game without rules which, to avoid confusion, I call Elyball.

If I were to tee it up with someone playing Elyball, therefore, in my terms, I am playing golf and he or she is playing something else.

The marketing campaign identifies a "fun" element experienced with a club that slingshots the ball extraordinary distances. That seems to me to lead to consideration of also using non-conforming balls (so-called "hot balls") which are available and go considerably greater distances with a given amount of energy input than balls which conform to the Rules. There is reason to believe that using a club with maximum slingshot effect and the optimum hot ball would figuratively put the ball into orbit.

The marketing campaign for Elyball also refers to something called "recreational golf" as distinguished from "competitive golf." For me, at least, the term recreational golf has no meaning, because there are no rules to define it.

There is a case to be made for bifurcating the game into two games, e.g., "competitive golf" and "recreational golf." Doing so, however, requires rules, including rules which set standards for the equipment with which it is played, to define what is recreational golf and a governing authority to make and interpret those rules. I would not advocate such bifurcation, because I prefer one game with each of us developing our skills in relation to the skills of all others who play that game.

The advocates of Elyball take comfort from the fact that the ERC II is not deemed to be a non-conforming club wherever the R&A rules are applied. Consideration of that development needs to take account of how it evolved. When the USGA undertook to develop a standard to deal with spring-like effect, the R&A announced that it would also do so, but would develop a more pragmatically useful test. When, after some two years of effort, no such test was developed, the R&A, incomprehensibly, announced that there would be no test and that the clubs that would have been tested, including the ERC II, did not add enough distance to pose a problem for the game.

That distressing development needs to be evaluated with regard to two factors. One is that players are encouraged to pay megabucks for the ERC II on the premise that they are buying *a lot* of distance. The other is that the R&A has a rule in its Rule book which makes clubs with clubheads producing spring-like effect illegal and no standard to identify what constitutes proscribed spring-like effect.

Some way must be found out of the dilemma and the threat to the game posed by those developments. I fervently hope that the current bearers of the torch that was lit in 1754 will have the wit and the will to find it.

Vietnam War Protesters at the 1972 Open

An extraordinary development severely complicated the last round of the 1972 U.S. Open at Pebble Beach. Late in the day with five pairs still on the course, a group of about fifteen protesters broke from the gallery alongside the 18th fairway and ran out to the first of two trees in the fairway in the drive zone. They had a long chain to which each of them was attached. They located themselves and the chain in a circle around the tree, joined the two ends of the chain with a lock and disposed of the key. They then, more or less in unison, and in a sort of chant, began loudly expressing their protests concerning the Vietnam war.

That episode posed a unique problem to those responsible for the conduct of the Open. The five pairs still on the course included everyone with a reasonable chance of winning the Open. The tee shots on 18 of everyone of these players was either going to come to rest among the protesters or so close to them that their voluble presence would create a severe distraction. It was a formidable chain, so that a special saw would be required to break it and the sawing would take some time. The time consumed in locating such a saw and sawing the chain precluded that option.

None of the other options provided a totally effective solution.

The first USGA official to react was Joe Dey, who had been the Executive Director of the USGA and continued to be an important rulings and other resource in the conduct of the Open. Joe was so incensed at this intrusion into the sanctified atmosphere of the Open that he took leave of his senses. Carrying his shooting stick like a billy club, he headed toward the protesters, apparently bent on bashing the lot of them. It is daunting to think what the consequences could have been had he not been physically restrained by another official.

Harry Easterly was Chairman of the Championship Committee and therefore bore the ultimate responsibility for the conduct of that Open. Harry combined the qualities of a passionate lover of the game and the discipline, decisiveness and courage of an ex-Marine. He suspended play long enough to implement his plan which he had perceived with remarkable dispatch. He mobilized in the area of the 18th green a contingent of officials to whom he announced his plan. He then led us down the 18th fairway toward the scene of the crime. As I reflect on that experience, I am amused at the recollection that we literally marched with Easterly in the lead, reminiscent of a Marine platoon on its way to take out an enemy gun emplacement.

When we arrived at the scene of the crime, Harry placed us in a line on the bay side of the tree as close as possible to the protesters without making physical contact. Harry's plan was to use us as a buffer, screening players whose drives were hit into the desired area between the tree and the bay from movement by the protesters and, to some extent, from any noise they might make.

Harry then stationed himself on the 18th tee and directed play to resume. He advised each pair of the situation and said they simply would have to deal with it as best they could.

Harry never said what he would have done if a ball had ended up among the protesters. In view of the effectiveness of his decisive leadership, it is only right that each of the players hit his drive elsewhere than among the protesters and Harry was saved from a decision for which centuries of precedent did not provide a clue.

As a footnote to that episode, the protesters were left chained around the tree and it was some hours into the night after the course was deserted of players and spectators before they were sawed free.

Jerry Pate and Plain English

In the 1977 Open played at Southern Hills, Jerry Pate pushed his tee shot on the 18th hole deep into the woods. His ball came to rest between a cart path and a large tree. Jerry took the position that he intended to play the shot left handed, which meant that he would be standing on the cart path and, therefore, would be entitled to relief from that obstruction. Having been denied relief by the official working that hole, Jerry appealed. That brought me into the scene.

As I saw the situation, there was no reasonable possibility that Jerry would have elected to play that shot left handed if the cart path had not been there. In attempting to express that point of view to Jerry, I began to ramble a bit with comments about totally changing the configuration of the shot and perceived problems attending an attempt to play the shot left handed. When I finally finished my analysis, Jerry said, "Sandy, I understand that you got a degree from Oxford University. I barely made it through Alabama. Would you mind putting what you just said in plain English so that I can understand it?" I managed to summarize my dissertation in plain English, to wit, "You are not entitled to relief, Jerry." Communication having been so effected, Jerry proceeded gracefully to deal with the problem his lousy tee shot had posed for him.

Death Threat

The 1977 U.S. Open at Southern Hills had a distressingly dramatic element added by a death threat that was received during the play of the last round. The threat was directed at Hubert Green, who was then in the lead.

It was expressed in a telephone call from a woman received by the Chief of Security. She said she was calling because her boyfriend and another man were en route to Southern Hills to shoot Hubert when he reached the 15th green and she wanted to alert security in the hope that such a tragedy for all concerned could be prevented.

The threat had an eerie validity, because not only was the 15th green the only place on that golf course where a shot fired from outside the course could hit someone on the course, but the hillside behind that green from which such a shot could be fired had on it two empty houses under construction affording total cover for the shooter.

As Chairman of the USGA Championship Committee I was in charge of that Open and responsible, therefore, for the decision of what to do in these circumstances.

Hubert was playing the 10th hole when I was told about the threat. The options as I saw them were morbidly fascinating:

1. Cancel the Open;
2. Suspend play for the day;
3. Suspend play until we could secure the area;
4. Do what we could in the time remaining before Hubert reached that green to secure the area and give Hubert the option of withdrawing or proceeding to play after he played the 14th hole.

The security measures adopted were impressive, including surveillance of the area, commandeering television cameras for surveillance, infiltrating the gallery with plain clothed police, and stationing armed police at appropriate places. To the extent possible these measures needed to be accomplished without creating unnecessary alarm.

Having satisfied myself that the area was secure, I decided on the number 4. option with the additional factor that Hubert would be given whatever reasonable time he needed to make his decision.

The problem of communicating with Hubert was complicated by two factors. One was to do so away from the considerable gallery, and the other was the Chief of Security being convinced that the call was a gambler's ploy hoping to upset Hubert. The Chief, therefore, was adamantly opposed to telling Hubert.

I finally had to pull rank so that the Chief reluctantly accompanied me when I took Hubert aside in a stand of trees where there was no gallery alongside the 14th green after he had putted out.

I told Hubert that the Chief had received a telephone call the content of which Hubert should hear and asked the Chief to repeat what he had been told. The Chief with manifest reluctance proceeded to do so but instead of saying that she had said he would be shot, the Chief substituted the word "hurt." I said, "Come on, Chief, Hubert is entitled to hear it exactly as you heard it." The Chief then said, "Well she said they are going to shoot you!" Hubert, who has extraordinarily large very dark eyes, opened these eyes very wide and said, "Shoot me? Did you say that was a woman who made that call? You don't think that is someone I have been taking out, do you?" That response certainly reduced the tension. Hubert opted to go on without delay.

He then proceeded to hit an awful snap hook drive on 15 that fortunately struck a tree and came back out of the woods but into an awkward lie alongside a bunker. He then hit a wonderful shot which finished on the green about 40 feet from the hole.

On the way to the green I alerted the other player and the two caddies about the telephone threat. When we reached the green they managed to clear out summarily so that as Hubert was taking an awfully long time to surveil his difficult 40 foot putt, there was no one else on the green but me and Hubert.

He managed to get down in two putts and somehow regain the intensity of his focus on winning the Open. He did so by making a birdie on 16 which gave him a two-shot lead and the cushion he needed.

His reaction in the following press conference was reluctance to talk about it which, I understand, has been his reaction ever since.

The War
Between the States
as a Factor

Hubert Green was also involved in another rules problem at Southern Hills in 1977. He buried a ball in the face of a bunker so that the sand completely covered his ball without leaving any indication of where in the face of the bunker the ball was located. The Rules accommodate such a situation by allowing Hubert to go into the bunker and work over the sand surface until he locates his ball, providing he does so within five minutes of starting the search. Hubert knew that rule, but, before he started his search, he had the wit to ask a question not then covered by the Rules; namely, whether, after he had located his ball and before he played the next shot from there, he could repair the footprints and other damage done to the sand surface in the course of his search for his ball. It was a perfectly sensible question, because there was a distinct possibility that the ball was so buried that he would not be able to extricate it from the bunker, and, when he played the shot, the ball would fall back into one of the deep footprints he had made in the course of the search.

The official who was at the scene referred the question to the Rules Committee for the Championship, which consisted of me and two southerners. The three of us were located at different places around the course so that we had to deal with the question on the radio intercom. We had a suitably spirited discussion in which I took the position that Hubert should be permitted to restore the bunker to the condition in which he had found it before he started his search and the two southerners took the position that he could not. Unable to persuade my colleagues to reach what I then thought and still think was the right result, I asked, over the radio, the official on the scene whether he had heard the discussion. He said that he had, so I told him to go ahead and give Hubert the decision.

Sometime later, someone who had been at the scene and had heard the discussion over the radio, located me and said, "Didn't the three of you decide that Hubert could not restore the pre-search condition of the bunker?" I said, "Yes, while I think it was wrong, that was the 2-1 decision." My informant then said, "Well, that was not what the official told Hubert; he told Hubert that he could restore the pre-search condition of the bunker!"

The scene then shifts to a discussion between me and the official as follows:

Me: Arthur (which was his name), what decision did you give
          Hubert about restoring the condition of that bunker?
Arthur: I told him he could restore the condition.
Me: Didn't you hear the discussion between me and Harry
          and P.J.? (At this point, it is pertinent to point out that
          Arthur was from Boston with a most pronounced
          Bostonian accent.)
Arthur: Yes, I heard the discussion, but I could not understand
          one word that those mush-mouth southerners were
          saying; you were the only one I could understand!

There was a case, therefore, where Hubert Green and justice were the beneficiaries of a remnant of the war between the States.

Infractions Observed
on Television

There has been some interesting controversy over rules infractions observed by people watching television who called in their observations to tournament committees, with disastrous consequences to some players who had violated the rules.

There was, for example, the celebrated incident of Craig Stadler in a tour event being recorded on television building a stance with a towel to protect his trousers while playing a shot in a kneeling position from under a tree. Stadler, apparently unaware that he had violated a rule, failed to add the penalty he incurred to his score so that, by signing his scorecard, he certified a score that was lower than that which he had in fact made. The consequence of that additional rules infraction was disqualification.

There also was an incident involving Paul Azinger, who in the process of taking a stance in a water hazard, cleared away some loose impediments with his foot. Apparently unconscious of the fact that he had violated a rule, Azinger also failed to add the penalty to his score on the hole and suffered the consequences when the infraction was identified.

In each of those incidents, the rules infraction was not identified on the golf course, but rather had been observed by someone watching television who had called tournament headquarters to apprise the officials of the infraction.

The controversy that developed from such incidents included a lot of sympathy for the players involved on the basis that it was unfair to have such additional television surveillance of leading players while players who did not have such television coverage were free of such surveillance.

While not wanting to appear insensitive to the draconian consequences visited on the players involved, I must say that the unfairness argument misses the fundamental point.

One of golf's features is that each player is personally responsible for the accuracy of the score he records on each hole. The score necessarily includes not only the number of times that he has hit the ball, but also the number of penalties strokes, if any, that he has incurred along the way. Obviously, such responsibility includes both an understanding of the rules and being sufficiently conscious of them so that the player is aware when he incurs a penalty. There is no good reason why that responsibility should be affected in any way by the fact that the player is or is not being covered by television. In the final analysis, it is the player's responsibility and if he fails to meet it, he should suffer the consequences.

There is a related question of whether the consequences are too draconian. That question was dramatically illuminated when Roberto di Vicenzo certified a scorecard recording a wrong score on the next to the last hole of The Masters in 1968 so as to deprive Roberto of a tie for first. In that case Roberto was not disqualified, because the score that he had certified was more than the score he had in fact made and the rule in those circumstances is that he was simply charged with the score he recorded rather than the score he made.

There is good reason for a different rule for recording a higher score than the rule applied for recording a lower score than you made. The reason is concerned with the necessity for a point of finality; that is, the time when the score you record becomes final and cannot be adjusted. While arguments can be made for some other time, it is not unreasonable to make that time the point at which the player certifies his score by signing his card and turning it into the officials. Accepting the premise that thereafter the score cannot be adjusted, it seems to me to that there is good reason for the difference in the rules. The player who records the higher score than he made does not negatively affect the result for any other player, whereas there is no fair way to allow the lower score to stand.

In the context of this discussion, the personal responsibility element in the playing of the game deserves reemphasis. The integrity of the game is dependent upon this feature. Each of us has to bear that responsibility. That responsibility certainly includes recording, as a part of our score, any penalty strokes we incurred; and in golf, as in life, ignorance of the law cannot be a valid excuse.

The State
of the Game

A Valedictory

When my term (1978-80) as President of the USGA was ending , I wrote a valedictory on *The State Of The Game* which was published in the *Golf Journal*. As I view what I then wrote, it seems to me to have currency. I reproduce some parts of it here which are not covered elsewhere in this book, therefore, as being a current statement of my views:

> *I have deep feelings about golf. I have often asked myself why I should feel so deeply about a game that I have tried for so long and with such fervor to learn, and yet have never come close to accomplishing. (I find that the caring intensifies as the prospect of accomplishment diminishes.) The answer lies beyond my comprehension. Parts of it, certainly, involve the soul-stirring satisfaction of playing a golf shot precisely as one has envisioned it. Partly, too, there are the stimuli given to the senses by the aroma of a freshly cut course early on a spring morning, the sight of a beautifully designed hole, the camaraderie among companions who share one's feelings, and the sense of achievement that follows a round played somewhere near one's capability. I am a dreamer, and dreamers are especially responsive to golf. If anyone doubts this, I refer him to Michael Murphy's book* Golf in the Kingdom *or to Bernard Darwin's essay "The Links of Eiderdown."*
>
> *Golf also tends to evoke strong feelings. I was a witness, for example, to an illustrative scene on the 11th tee at Cypress Point. A four-ball was in progress involving Pat Ward-Thomas, who wrote superbly on golf for so many years for* The GUARDIAN *newspaper, in England, and Alistair Cooke. Alistair hit what can*

charitably be described as a rather tentative tee shot that man-
aged only barely to avoid a bunker. That fortuitous result having
been commented upon by the assemblage, Ward-Thomas fixed
us with a contemptuous glare and said, "When I hit a lousy shot,
the last thing I want is condolences. The only suitable reaction is
dead silence!" He then teed up his ball, renewed the glare and
said, "Furthermore, the worst thing that anyone can say is, 'It's
only a game. The hell it's only a game!" Whereupon with un-
bridled passion he poured body and soul into his tee shot.

Strong feelings evoke strong views.

In late January, (1980) I leave the Executive Committee of
the United States Golf Association after several gratifying years
laboring to promote and preserve the game. I find this, therefore,
a moment for reflection upon what I have seen and what I fore-
see. As you examine these reflections, I hope you will be indulgent
about some personal and rather emphatic views I have on some
controversial subjects.

The maintenance of golf courses in this country is a key factor
in how the game has developed here. Maintenance generally, as I
see it, is deteriorating. This is a paradox in view of the twin facts
that the means for proper maintenance are improving and that
increasing numbers of golf course superintendents are trained
agronomists. The problem, simply put, is one of too much water!
This has been endemic to this country for a long time. As the game
here came more and more to be played in the air, with bounce and
roll relatively negligible factors, heavily watered golf courses
became easily justified. As a related factor, we seem to care more
about how a golf course looks than about how it plays. The lush
green look has become more than the norm; it has become the stan-
dard. It is, moreover, much easier to maintain a lush green look.

The game in this country, therefore, has largely become a slog
from one mushy lie to another, with greens that will hold vir-
tually any sort of a shot however struck and which are so slow they
can be putted with relative impunity, because the misjudged or

miss-hit putt will not go very far.

For ages the Old Course at St. Andrews provided the classic example of the Scottish game. I use the past tense because today the Old Course is nothing like it was 30 years ago when I had the thrill of playing it for the first time. The character of the Old Course is being destroyed by water. In the 1978 British Open, for example, 180-yard iron shots were backing up on those greens! That wondrously subtle necessity of hitting the tee shot to precisely the right place to be able to get at the hole with the approach shot was virtually gone. While I believe that this condition is becoming progressively worse, it is not a new development. Herbert Warren Wind told me that when Bob Jones came back to St. Andrews, in 1958, with the American team for the first World Amateur Team Championship, he remarked that much of the fire and, therefore, the flavor, had gone out of the Old Course.

All of this leads to some thoughts about Augusta National. It moves me profoundly to see in such a superb setting a piece of ground that shows what Bob Jones perceived to be the game of golf. One of the many fascinating aspects of Augusta National is the unmistakable influence of the Old Course on its design (the Old Course, that is, as it was when Jones played it). Like the Old Course, the efficacy of Augusta's design depends upon the firmness and pace of the greens.

As money more and more becomes the name of the game in virtually every sport played in this country, I become concerned over the influence money could have on the future of golf. Obviously, a lot has happened already. Public and press attention is so focused on those who play for prize money that the essence of the game is lost among statistics showing who won how much. Some risks are inherent, too, in the heavy proportion of skilled young players who grow up in an environment that is directed toward the singular objective of playing golf for money. When the game is properly administered, nothing is wrong with playing golf for money. The concern, however, is that the game, which has so much to offer as a game to be played for its own sake, becomes something else as it evolves primarily into a medium for making money.

Golf, at least up to this point, has not had visited upon it the sorts of scenes that are increasingly afflicting men's tennis. That problem is the direct consequence of money so dominating a sport that the people who play it become more important than the game they play. In this sense, certainly, golf has retained its character. The dominant figures in the game—the Palmers, the Nicklauses and the Watsons, for example—have maintained a solid balance between a sense of their own importance and the importance of the game that has provided them with the premises for their importance. Anyone who cares about golf ought to pray that this will continue to be so.

One disturbing element in this picture involves the United States Open Championship. The atmosphere of the Open becomes increasingly afflicted by some players who complain too much. The heart of the game is missing when it is played in such a frame of mind.

That the heart of the game can be preserved in the context of playing it for money is best illustrated by the final round of the 1978 Women's Open Championship. JoAnne Carner and Hollis Stacy were paired together. Never more than a stroke separated them throughout the day. Hollis won the Championship by holing an excruciatingly difficult putt after JoAnne had put it to her by holing one that was even more difficult. I was privileged to referee that round. It was perhaps the most exuberant example I have ever seen of extracting from the game all of the joy that can be in it and transmitting that joy to those who saw it. It has been truly said that the spirit of amateurism (that is, playing a game for the sheer love of it) is not a function of whether prize money is involved, but rather of the spirit with which the game is played.

Nonetheless, it seems to me that all the historical and traditional reasons for preserving the distinction between the amateur and the professional continue to be valid. As commercialism pro-

gressively consumes sport, it becomes more important to have the game played for its own sake, rather than for the revenue that can be produced. The spirit as well as the concept of amateurism in golf need all the nurturing we can give them. In doing so, we will have to deal somehow with a pervasive problem that is afflicting the amateur game in this country. As college golf becomes increasingly competitive and as increasing numbers of good young players use college golf scholarships as a means of preparing for professional golf careers, serious competitive imbalance is affecting amateur golf at every level—at the club level, at the state and regional level, and at the national level. Someone who plays the game avocationally, particularly someone who works for a living, simply cannot compete with a good young college golfer who spends a disproportionate part of his time working on his game and playing in the flood of intensely competitive golf events that make up the college golf scene. We need to find a way to restore competitive balance in amateur golf, particularly for those who do in fact play the game as an avocation.

The importance of amateurism in golf involves more than the spirit. My experience with the inner workings of the administration of the game has confirmed not just the validity but also the critical importance of having knowledgeable, dedicated amateurs determine and interpret the Rules of Golf. This keeps the emphasis where it belongs— on the fundamental fact that golf is a game to be played for its own sake. The rules-making function must be rooted in that fact and must not be influenced by what may or may not be the commercial consequences of a given Rule or its interpretation.

Television could be a prime medium for developing an understanding of the Rules. We have begun to use it, but we have a long way to go to realize the effectiveness of this tool. It has limitless potential for developing interest in the game, but it is not being used properly. Golf suffers from too many poorly produced telecasts. Commentary is a pervasive problem because too much is

133

said about too little. Audio should merely supplement the camera; it should provide only information the viewer needs to understand the full picture. A good deal has been done, first by ABC and then by NBC to improve telecasts of USGA events; that progress provides encouragement that we can realize what we should from this medium.

Notwithstanding all my concerns, I move on into the pastures where past presidents roam with confidence that golf will make it through a difficult future in a complex world with its quality and character intact. The intrinsic beauty and fascination of the game will continue to inspire people to preserve it. There are an extraordinary number of effective people who care profoundly about it.

My involvement during these past two years (1978-80) has taken me from Fiji to St. Andrews and many places in between. It has been an indescribable experience. I leave such involvement with a love of the game that I know is shared by people everywhere I have been. A game that evokes such a universal response should be able to withstand anything—even golf carts and unconscionable amounts of water.

Insidious Intrusions

As the game of golf has evolved, there have been some insidious intrusions into the purity of spirit that should ennoble all True Believers in the True Game. The True Game, of course, simply involves teeing it up on the first tee and proceeding to play in accordance with the Rules that define the game.

One insidious intrusion into that pristine pure concept is the so-called "mulligan," the name applied to the practice of permitting the player who has driven unsatisfactorily from the first tee to hit a second drive. That practice has further been adulterated in some misguided circles by permitting the player to choose which of the two balls he will play for his second shot!

It was a player by the name of David Mulligan whose name identifies this infamous practice. It is a modest bit of comfort to note that he was a Canadian and, therefore, in a sense, not one of us. That comfort is offset, however, by the fact that this insidious practice originated at, of all places, Winged Foot Golf Club, which has a great golf course where a wonderful lot of the history of the game in this country has been made.

David Mulligan moved to New York and became a member of Winged Foot in 1937. The recorded history of that club includes the following item:

"Mulligan played a fair game, but he was, as they say, a slow starter. His drive off the first tee oft went astray. Turning plaintively to his friends he would plead, or perhaps only look, saying 'Another?'" Being generous souls they would nod, permissively, if not enthusiastically. David is remembered by our senior members today for his warmth, and the pleasure he had while sitting in the lounge with his Scotch and soda, proudly claiming credit for golf's most generous gesture, the mulligan."

Such blasphemy should have at least caused him to choke on his Scotch and soda, particularly when you consider that the True Game is our heritage from the Scots.

As bad developments are inclined to do, they spawn something worse. The mulligan has led to an aberration called Hit 'til Happy. In the outlaw circles where this practice is permitted, players remain on the first tee hitting the shots with abandon until they hit one that makes them happy! I once engaged in a brief discussion with a practitioner of this aberrational behavior. I countered his claim for the benefits of this nonsense by noting that he and I simply had a fundamental difference in that his premise is that the round starts in the middle of the first fairway whereas mine is that the round starts on the first tee.

While there are other misguided intrusions into the True Spirit of the True Game, suffice it to say here that David Mulligan and his progeny, the Hitters 'til Happy, should be relegated to the Hall of Shame.

The most pervasive of all such intrusions is the practice of playing so-called *winter rules*.

It is distressing to think how the Scots, to whom all of us hooked on golf are deeply indebted for creating this game, would view the concept that golf is a seasonal game only played in the summer and that in the winter players play some other game in which they move the ball to the best lie they can manage to find in the vicinity.

As we consider such nonsense and how intrusive this practice has become in this country, we should duly consider our heritage and how it should influence us to mend our ways.

An impressive illustration of our forebears' approach to the game is provided by a club they used called the rut iron. That was a club with a head configuration designed to help the player play the ball from a wagon wheel rut. Now that tells you a lot about the robust approach that our ancestors took to the playing of this game. There was a pervasive element of character in that approach; that is, accepting personal responsibility for having hit the ball into whatever lie in which it came to rest. There also was the fundamental premise that in golf, as in life, you took whatever were the consequences of your act, however much bad luck may have been involved in those consequences, and simply dealt with them as best as you could.

Evaluating the merits of our ancestors' approach, should help to face up to the real premises for so-called winter rules. The Rules of Golf make no reference to winter rules. Such rules are dealt with in a suggested local rule pertaining to "preferred lies." Such rule in effect reads that if a player can identify a lie he prefers to the one into which he hit his ball, he is entitled to place his ball in the preferred lie! How can such a concept be squared with any sensible premise for the playing of the game of golf?

The most heinous departure from the true spirit of the playing of the game is the preferred lie rule practiced by the PGA Tour. The Tour has a rule applied in Tour events in circumstances, as I have observed them, of remarkably benign damp conditions allowing the player to lift and place his ball in any lie which he prefers no nearer the hole and within one club length of the lie into which he hit his ball. I observed an illustration of what a lousy rule that is some years ago playing in The Crosby with Tom Watson. We were paired with Jay Haas playing Spyglass Hill. On the 10th hole, Jay hit his tee shot up against the base of one of the trees standing in the fairway on that hole. With the Tour preferred lie rule in effect, Jay simply extricated himself without penalty from that impossible position into which he had hit the ball by moving it one club length and placing it so that he had a problem free approach to the green.

The Tour on occasion takes this nonsense to the ultimate nonsense of making the relief available through the green, *i.e.*, everywhere but in a hazard, and, most notably, in the rough! I cannot imagine what the premise is for allowing a player, and most especially a professional, who has failed to hit the fairway to find a friendly tuft of grass in the rough on which to give himself a driver lie.

One of the alleged premises for playing the preferred lie game is that it promotes fairness. The nonsense of that premise is illustrated by the Jay Haas incident. As Jack Nicklaus put it, "Whoever said that golf was supposed to be fair!"

There are multiple good reasons for playing the game in the true spirit bequeathed to us by our Scot forbears and many bad reasons for turning golf into some other game.

Abominable Intrusions

One feature of the game that has taken an awful turn for the worse is the increasingly pervasive use of so-called "golf carts." As this development began to take hold in this country, I wrote a piece on the subject which was published in *Golf Digest*. As this perverse development continues to proliferate, I am moved to reaffirm those views by republishing them here:

> *When the Industrial Revolution finally caught up with the game of golf as played on the Old Course at St. Andrews, it did so in the form of a vehicle to replace the caddie. The vehicle had two wheels, a handle and a device for holding the golf bag so that the player could comfortably pull it behind him as he walked. The British called these vehicles "trollies." As the tale is told, the trolley was introduced at St. Andrews by one of the older members, who for many years had regularly played the Old Course with a friend of like vintage. The first time the old boy showed up with the thing, there was a noticeable void in the group that left the first tee, because, while the friend had his regular caddie, the old boy's caddie had been replaced by the trolley. When the game reached the first green, the old boy's ball was a long way from the hole, so he asked the friend's caddie to hold the flagstick for him. The caddie, with that special note of disdain that can only be struck by one of the older St. Andrews caddies, replied, "If ye want tha flagstick held, have tha thing that's carryin' yer bag hold it!"*
>
> *The incident illustrates two of the many deficiencies of devices designed to transport bags around the course. The are utterly devoid of personality and there are critical functions they simply cannot perform.*
>
> *Characteristically, the intrusion of the Industrial Revolution into the*

game of golf in our country has gone far beyond the trolley, to motorized cars designed to transport not just the golf bag but two bags and two players.

Golf carts are a peculiarly American development. Their impact on the game of golf in this country has been overwhelming. Whether that has been good or bad for the game depends on the point of view. Mine is that it has been devastatingly bad.

At the outset of explaining that view, a basic premise should be understood. Golf carts have been a positive development for people who could not play without them. Their use by such people obviously is more than justifiable—it is a necessity. But those people comprise a small percentage of golfers. It is the use of these things by people who do not need them that is fouling the game.

There are many compelling reasons why somehow golf carts must be exorcised. They eliminate walking the course. That is akin to taking the mountains out of skiing. They are converting golf into a sedentary sport. A sadder demise cannot be imagined for a game developed by the hardy Scots testing the elements on the links along the Scottish coasts.

Walking, particularly on a beautiful course, provides its own element of pleasure. Mark Twain went so far as to say, "Golf is a good walk spoiled." Walking does much more than provide useful exercise. The pleasure in it can provide solace to the search for the ball mis-hit into the woods; it can add zest to the triumph of a long-iron shot that finishes near the hole.

Proper pace and rhythm in walking the course can give crucial assistance to instilling the optimum tempo into the golf swing. Bouncing and jerking around the premises in one of those infernal machines minimizes the possibility of finding consistent rhythm.

Approaching the next shot at a sensible pace on foot also gives the player the proper time and perspective to contemplate what the shot will require and how he will deal with it.

Walking is conducive to the spirit of camaraderie that characterizes golf. Moving through the course on foot with your partner and competitors provides the setting for the sort of discourse that means so much to the pleasure of playing the game. Segregated in carts, the players meet sporadically on the greens and tees and have no chance to sustain the sort of leisurely conversation stimulated by the environment of the game.

Golf courses usually are lovely places where the senses are stimulated. Golf carts foul that environment. All of them clutter up the scene. They are out of place and they look it. Many of them pollute the air with gasoline fumes and clobber the atmosphere with noise. Riding in one of them on a lovely golf course is like traversing a pristine snow covered meadow in the Sierra on a snowmobile.

Among golf's many distinctions is the beauty of the places where it is played. The feelings engendered by the visual impact of a golf course have a lot do to with how much or how little stimulus the player derives from a round of golf. Golf carts require cart paths, which permeate the landscape. These black blotches are ugly intrusions into the scenery. They also afflict the game with aberrational bounces and ridiculous rulings.

The visual aspects of the use of these machines include the sight, both slightly sad and comic, of two somewhat overweight men in their prime years climbing into one of the things and racing down the fairway.

However fast the things go, they inevitably slow up the playing of the game. Maneuvering from one player's ball to the other, problems of getting the cart in the right position so that the player can determine what club he needs for his shot and then getting his club and then returning it to the cart and then getting back in and then heading for his partner's ball where the whole process is repeated, all combine to more than offset the speed with which the players can race from one point to another.

A proliferation of these things on golf courses all over the country has virtually extinguished the caddie. Caddies gave the game a personal dimension that added something these monsters simply cannot provide.

Caddying, moreover, provided access to golf for countless youngsters who otherwise would have had no exposure to it. This once was the prime source of the better players. It provided the game with the likes of Sarazen, Hagen, Hogan and Nelson. To have come to golf through that route not only provided the player with special skills, it gave him a special respect for the game.

Caddie programs contribute significantly to communities where clubs and courses are located. They introduce young people to a useful game

while providing them with income and healthful activity in attractive sur-
roundings. This country can use all such programs it can get for its young
people. These programs are practically the only means of getting young peo-
ple from low and moderate income families interested in the game. When
you consider how much effort the PGA of America, for one, puts into pro-
moting junior golf, you have to wonder why it should not be putting at
least a like effort into promoting constructive caddie programs.

Caddies, of course, receive the bag-carrying revenue, whereas golf cart
revenue goes to the proprietor. There is a pervasive view that the revenue
generated by golf carts justifies their use. For golfers to submit to that view
is analogous to the residents of Williamsburg, Virginia, deciding to reduce
their taxes by establishing gambling casinos on the main street. How can
anything so destructive be justified as an economic necessity? A modest
amount of imagination can deal with replacing whatever revenue incre-
ment may be involved in their use.

These machines actually make golf more expensive for all of us. If the
game is to prosper, the expense connected with it has to be reduced. Any
cost analysis must account for the awful amount of energy these things con-
sume.

Caddies are nonexistent at America's resort courses. Virtually all resorts
require players to use golf carts in order to raise revenue. This is a wrong
reason for confining the players to carts. The revenue could be replaced by
a fee for a properly designed pullcart. Golf courses could be improved by
the elimination of cart paths and money could be saved on maintenance.
The players' enjoyment would be enhanced.

All of the people who are promoting golf, for whatever purpose, ought
to take a critical look at how golf carts are affecting their respective inter-
ests. When they review what carts do for the game against what carts do to
it, they ought to conclude that there are a number of better ways to get a
golf bag around a golf course and that everybody's (but the golf cart man-
ufacturers') interests would be served by confining the use of those things to
people who could not play without a machine to transport them. People
who think it is impossible to exorcise the things from the game should real-
ize that nothing is impossible when so much can be done for so many with

the eminently sensible solutions that are available. With regard to all the problems of readjusting to a walking game, we should have the attitude of the octogenarian who when asked how he coped with the vicissitudes of age replied, "It beats the alternative."

Playing the game in a cart simply is not and cannot be golf. We need a name for it. I suggest "cart-ball." I also suggest that anyone who uses a cart unnecessarily cannot be called a golfer (a "cart-baller"?) and a club that promotes or permits their indiscriminate use cannot be a golf club (a "cart-ball club"?).

When I play golf occasionally in the UK and France and observe the increasing use of "buggies" in the UK and golf carts in France, I am moved to muse about how salutary it could be if the United Nations could develop a global golf cart non-proliferation treaty to save the game from those abominable machines.

Any reference to the use of carts necessarily leads to consideration of the Casey Martin case. Obviously, no one can or should prevent Casey from using a cart when he plays the game that cart users play. The issue that Casey's case has framed, however, is whether walking is an integral part of the playing of the game of golf. Based on my experience of more than 70 years playing the game I do not just believe, I know, that it is.

Consideration of the issue understandably has been complicated by sympathy. The sympathy factor has been intensified by how serious, painful and debilitating is Casey's affliction and by how exemplary and attractive he is. That factor has so overwhelmed consideration of other factors that anyone expressing the view that walking is an integral part of playing golf has been subjected to an awful lot of calumny, particularly by the media.

A dispassionate view of the matter, however, identifies just two questions. One is whether endurance and fatigue related to walking are important factors in playing golf. I know that they are. While my knowledge convinces me, I would not presume that it could be persuasive in the broader arena. What is, as I see it, conclusively persuasive in that arena is the experience and related knowledge of golfers such as Arnold Palmer, Jack Nicklaus, Ken Venturi and the conclusive majority of golfers who make their living playing stroke play golf for prize money.

The other question is whether the United States government should be determining what the requirements are for the playing of a sport rather than the sport's governing body. I cannot see how anyone can seriously conclude that the government is the better authority.

I have no problem with anyone who wants to organize cart ball competitions or in having the governing body of golf also govern that game and such competitions, but the pervading fact is that that game simply is not golf.

Since the foregoing was written the Supreme Court has decided the Casey Martin case. The media analyses of the Supreme Court decision I have read or heard did not go beyond smug satisfaction that the rock-solid, lame kid knocked over the rich, arrogant, soulless establishment. But the issues in the case are more complex—and potentially far-reaching—than that.

The threshold issue is whether the Americans with Disabilities Act was intended to apply to professional sports. While the Supreme Court has now settled that issue as it pertains to golf, there was good reason to assert that it did—and should—not.

That decision casts the government in the role of dictating to sports' governing bodies what the requirements are for the playing of the games they govern. The Casey Martin case is a case in point.

The issue here was whether walking and related fatigue are material factors affecting performance results produced over 72 holes played in PGA Tour conditions. The Tour, confirmed by a very large majority of the players who actually experience those conditions, determined that such factors are material. And yet seven justices, some of whom play but in nothing like Tour conditions and in carts (which seems to me to make a fatigue point), determined that the Tour's game should be played according to the rules established by the justices. This decision is a casebook example of how hard cases can make bad law.

The U.S. Amateur
and
Amateur Golf

This championship certainly has been in the vanguard of the development of golf.

As one example, it was for the purpose of having an organization which could validate a national amateur champion that five golf clubs got together in 1894 and created The United States Golf Association. That provided the game in this country with a governing body of golf, one that combines in effect with the Royal and Ancient Golf Club of St. Andrews so that wherever golf is played around the world, the players are all playing the same game.

That first U.S. Amateur Championship was played in 1895 at The Newport Golf Club in Rhode Island. It attracted a field of 32 players. There have been championships played every year since 1895, excepting only the war years.

The 1999 championship attracted a field of 7,920 players. Sectional qualifying was held at 94 courses in 41 states to reduce the field to 312. Those 312 then played 36 holes of stroke play at two courses, Spyglass Hill and Pebble Beach, to reduce the field to 64, who then played match play at Pebble Beach to determine the 1999 U.S. Amateur Champion.

That champion, David Gossett, earned identification with his name engraved on the Havemeyer Trophy along with the names of a wonderful collection of great players who have won that championship, such as:

Charles B. Macdonald; Walter Travis; H. Chandler Egan; Jerome Travers; William Fownes, Jr.; Francis Ouimet; Chick Evans; Bobby Jones; Lawson Little; Johnny Goodman; Arnold Palmer; Bill Campbell; and Jack Nicklaus.

Naturally, the first championship was played at match play because that was the game predominantly played by amateurs. The next 69 championships were also decided in that format. In 1965 the format was changed to stroke play. After using that format for eight years, the USGA in 1973 rectified a bad decision by reverting the format to the match play game. We can be thankful that match play has been the format used ever since.

There are, of course, advocates for stroke play as the better format for identifying a champion. I prefer match play, particularly for amateurs, and if the decision were to be based on amateurs' preference reflected in the numbers who compete with each other at match play compared to those who choose stroke play, the vote for match play would be so overwhelming as to make counting votes a waste of time.

The winner of this championship is the champion amateur golfer of the United States. He ought to be so identified by playing the format that amateurs predominantly play.

Given the importance of amateur golf to the past, present and future development of the game, it is an anomaly that the media are so overwhelmingly focused on the professional game played for prize money. A visitor from outer space viewing our sports culture surely would conclude that this game called golf is only played by professionals playing stroke play for prize money. If, however, he were somehow to get beyond the media coverage of the game, he would learn that in comparison to the numbers of amateur players and the numbers of rounds they play, the related statistics for stroke play golf played for prize money makes that game relatively insignificant.

There is another much more important factor in recognizing the importance of amateur golf. Simply put, without the amateurs there would be no game of golf. They created the game, they nurtured it, they govern it, they make the rules that define the game, their play sustains the creation and the development of all the golf courses and it is they who, in the final analysis, provide the money that supports the professional game.

The word amateur derives from Greek words meaning, as a verb, to love and, as a noun, lover. That word, therefore, puts amateur golfers in the right frame of reference, because they are the lovers of it whose love provides the heart, and indeed the soul, of the game of golf.

Women's Golf

For many years, women in this country were the object of a demeaning advertising campaign with the theme "You've come a long way, baby!" The purpose of the campaign was to attract women to purported pleasures and status in smoking a particular brand of cigarette. When you consider the apparent success of the ad, judging from the years that it ran in all sorts of media, it is disturbing to contemplate how much cancer and heart trouble must have been a byproduct of the campaign.

As I have thought about that ad and the consequence of its success, it has occurred to me that there is a counterpart in the promotion of women's golf in this country by the United States Golf Association.

In 1895, when the USGA conducted the first amateur championship, it also identified the national champion of women's golf by organizing and conducting, in that same year, the first United States Women's Amateur Championship. That championship was played at Meadow Brook Club in Hempstead, New York and attracted a field of 13 women. In every year since, except for the war years, the USGA has continued to organize a U.S. Women's Amateur Championship.

As women came to play professional golf in sufficient numbers, in 1946 the USGA created the U.S. Women's Open Championship to identify the national champion of women's golf. Furthermore, women are entitled to enter both the U.S. Amateur Championship and the U.S. Open Championship if they have the requisite skill and choose to do so.

So the USGA has seen to it that women did not have to come a long way or indeed any distance at all to be in the vanguard of the game of golf in this country. It deserves emphasis that in promoting golf, the USGA necessarily promotes all the healthful benefits playing the game provides.

Senior Golf

For the older people in our population whom we call seniors, or more graciously senior citizens, golf is a Godsend. This is one game which provides pleasure, satisfaction, challenge and healthful exercise, the aging process notwithstanding. Indeed, it can be fairly said that golf is a life extender, both with respect to adding time to a player's lifespan and making the time approaching the end of life more useful and enjoyable.

It is no wonder, therefore, that the number of senior citizens playing the game is increasing exponentially and that so many continue to play and enjoy it in their eighties and indeed into their nineties.

Consistent with its role of promoting and preserving the game, the United States Golf Association was in the vanguard of recognizing the importance of senior golf when it established the United States Senior Open Championship first played at classic Winged Foot in 1980. This championship has continued to develop as one of the premier events in golf.

The quality of the play in this championship certainly provides a dramatic demonstration of how enduring are the skills of these players and of how much satisfaction in the playing of the best of all games remains for these senior citizens to enjoy.

Links Golf

The British Open continues to bring the visage of links golf onto our television screens. That setting takes the game back to its origins on the sandy wasteland left by the receding sea. Those stretches of non-arable land along the coasts of Scotland were viewed as linking the farmed land to the sea, so they became known as linksland. Since linksland was not arable and only marginally usable for grazing sheep, it provided a natural habitat for the playing of the game that came to be known as golf. The courses that evolved on linksland came to be known as links.

Those courses on which the game originated had distinctive characteristics. The terrain, while generally flat, had humps and hillocks created by the windblown sand. The courses evolved among those humps and hillocks with very little disturbance of the original terrain. The turfgrass that developed to form the playing surfaces was mostly a hardy strain of fescue and provided a firm playing surface so that there was considerable bounce and roll when the ball landed on it. The wind which helped to form the linksland was a fairly constant factor in the playing of the links courses.

The game that evolved, therefore, had related characteristics. The player had to calculate for a considerable amount of bounce and roll in playing a shot. The humps and hillocks complicated that calculation and injected a considerable element of chance into the outcome. The player also had to calculate how the wind was going to affect the flight, bounce and roll of the ball. Dealing with the wind also often dictated a low trajectory for a successful shot.

While the areas for greens were leveled off to some extent, they also had firm surfaces and undulations that affected the shots hit into them and added flavor to the problems of putting them.

That was the links game, the original game of golf. And that, at least to some extent, is still the game played on the classic courses on the coasts of the United Kingdom and Ireland.

As the game was brought across the Atlantic, some of the courses developed in this country were faithful to the game's origins, most notably Shinnecock Hills and The National on Long Island. Strangely, however, in view of what a wonderful game links golf is, as the game evolved over here the links' characteristics were lost and a very different game developed played from point to point in the air on lushly maintained, cemetery green courses.

The strangeness of that development is dramatized by the fact that players from the United States of all levels of skill, whose golf experience has been confined to the game played in the air, come back from pilgrimages to links courses in the British Isles uniformly ecstatic over the experience of playing links golf.

Tom Watson is the most famous—and by far the most successful—convert to links golf. His understanding and profound appreciation of that game had a lot to do with his winning five British Open championships. At a recent British Open, he was moved to make the following comment:

"Links golf demands that you use your imagination. In that respect it requires much more skill. The game in America is basically a game of hitting perfect shots fixed distances and seeing who makes the most putts. If you have 170 yards to the pin you take out a club, you hit the ball 165 yards and it stops dead on the green. That is target golf. In links golf, the target is always changing. When you are young you could not just knock an iron stiff. You did not play the game so much through the air as along the ground. You had to think about how the ground affected your shot. We don't do that much in America now. It is back to the cradle when you are playing links golf. That is why I love it so much."

I cannot improve on those sentiments. I can only wholeheartedly say amen and add one further note.

Links golf is linked to nature not just in the natural setting and evolution of the courses, but in the requirement of dealing with the elements. These elements, of course, include the wind and the rain. The weather used to be a further significant factor in that there were no irrigation systems, so the weather, determined how the course would play on any given day. Even in wet weather the courses were very firm. In dry weather they were, to use Bobby Jones' phrase, fiery.

As irrigation systems have been installed and agronomists have replaced greenkeepers and relied upon fertilizers, the fire has gone out of many of those classic courses. The links game is threatened with extinction.

A recent trip to play a number of those courses, however, has encouraged me to think that good sense is reasserting itself so that all is not lost.

The Old Course

The Old Course at St. Andrews in Scotland is frequently identified as "The Home of Golf." While the game may have originated elsewhere, there is no doubt that the identification effectively puts that God Given Place into proper perspective. That perspective was revived for me recently when I was privileged to be there for a few days. (Days there are always too few). There was for me indeed a distinct feeling of having come home.

I first saw and played the course in 1948. Airplanes and automobiles have taken a lot of the romance out of the homecoming to St. Andrews. In those days, the pilgrimage required that we board the train in London and travel overnight to Edinburgh and across The Firth of Forth to Leuchars Junction. There, transfer was made to an ancient train with a steam locomotive that, since there was no turnaround, backed down the several miles to St. Andrews. There was a point on that part of the journey where the track turned and the "auld grey town" came into view. The view shortly refined to the visage of the dunes, the humps, the hillocks and the gorse that make up the environs of The Old Course. Any True Believer, experiencing that scene at that turn in the track, instinctively anticipated the adventure and romance he was going to experience. It was that scene that provided the initial inspiration for Michael Murphy's book, *Golf in the Kingdom*.

The Old Course is, as it certainly should be, unique. No one designed it; it simply, and in a sense miraculously, evolved.

Perhaps the most remarkable of all its unique features is the enormous size of its greens. Seven of those greens accommodate two holes each with one played on the outgoing nine and one played on the incoming nine. Originally the course played out and back with the incoming holes played to the same hole as the outgoing holes. Increased volume of play, however, made this arrangement unworkable, so the greens were enlarged to accommodate two holes and the enlargement was sufficient so that play to one hole very seldom interferes with play to the other.

The course has a wonderful combination of humps, hillocks and bunkers. Many of the bunkers are penal pot bunkers and one of them, a very large one guarding the approach to the 14th green, is quite appropriately named "Hell Bunker."

The course has elicited—in some cases provoked—some extraordinary reactions from notable players. The immortal Bobby Jones tore up his card in disgust on the 11th green in his first British Open there in 1921. Jones subsequently developed a fervent love affair with the course and won his only British Amateur Championship there in 1930 in the process of achieving his never to be equaled "Grand Slam." That love affair is recorded in lyrical terms in Jones' writings about the game.

And then there was Sam Snead whose initial reaction was:

"We slowed past some acreage that was so raggedy and beat up that I was surprised to see what looked like a fairway among the weeds. Down home we wouldn't plant cow beats on land like that."

Snead proceeded, however, to win the 1946 British Open there, but nonetheless confirmed his initial impression by never coming back.

Sam's lack of vision caused him to miss what I believe to be the ultimate adventure a golfer can have and that is to experience the Old Course in all sorts of weather conditions that Scotland provides and to come to a true understanding of how endlessly fascinating the game of golf can be.

Some Golf
on The Old Course

On any list of matchless adventures that golf can provide, a round of golf on The Old Course has to be at or near the top. I recently had such an adventure in a round played there with Ernie Els, the young man from South Africa who has shown so much promise for a great career.

He confirmed that promise for me by playing The Old Course in a stiff north wind, which also was bitingly cold, in a brilliant 67. The combination of skills that were manifested in so conquering that golf course in those conditions can be properly described as awe inspiring.

Many years previously he had tried and failed to qualify for our Tour playing The Bayonet Course at what was Fort Ord in California. Particularly in view of his failure, I was impressed with his commentary on that course, to the effect that it was one of the better golf courses he had ever played.

That commentary revived for me some warm memories of the golf games I enjoyed many years ago with the amateur golfer who designed The Bayonet. He was an Army General stationed at Fort Ord named Bob McClure who played golf left handed with passionate feeling for the game. He invested a lot of that passionate feeling in the creation of that Bayonet Course as a heritage for all of us hooked on golf.

That round on The Old Course enjoyed with Ernie Els was played in a Pro-Am prelude to The Dunhill Cup. The Dunhill Cup was an extraordinary event created by Mark McCormack. It featured teams of three professional golfers from sixteen countries playing The Old Course in a modified match play format played on a team basis.

The United States Team that year consisted of an interesting trio, namely Fred Couples, John Daly and Payne Stewart. They won the event beating in the final an English team that included Nick Faldo, then the world's number one player.

It was John Daly's first exposure to The Old Course, with its unique features providing very different challenges from those with which he is accustomed to dealing. He handled both those challenges and himself with extraordinary effectiveness. As the final match evolved, it was up to Daly to win or lose it for the U.S.A. team. He played down the stretch with remarkable resolution on a very cold, windy day and on a golf course with very demanding requirements. It was an impressive performance, providing further promise that John Daly, if he somehow can control the demons that have afflicted his life, can make his mark as someone with much more to bring to the game than booming tee shots. That promise, of course, was affirmed, if momentarily, when he went on to win the 1995 British Open at St. Andrews. In contrast to Sam Snead, Daly seemed to enjoy his exposure to the vagaries of the game played on The Old Course.

So also did Payne Stewart, with whom I had an engaging conversation about the special experience that links golf provides in contrast to the point game played in the air in America.

George Bush, who is a member of the R&A, played The Old Course recently in the Club's premier event known as "The Autumn Medal." He was paired with Arnold Palmer, who also is a member. It was a brisk, windy day and President Bush made a respectable showing in relation to his handicap when he scored 42 on the first nine. I was playing in the event later that day. As I left the 10th tee, I said to my delightful Scot caddie, "Do you realize that you have the privilege of carrying the bag of a player who has just played the first nine holes on The Old Course in the same score as that recorded by the immediate past President of the United States?" He promptly replied in his inimitable brogue, "I thought of that, but I didn't think I should mention it!"

The U.S. Open

The U.S. Open is a true open championship, conducted to identify the national champion of golf in the country with the world's largest golfing population by several orders of magnitude.

The open character of this championship is one of its essential features. Anyone, male or female, citizen or alien, adult or juvenile, can play, with the singular requirement being the requisite skill. In 2001 8,398 players entered, and 116 qualifying events were conducted in 45 states.

The open feature of this championship over the years has provided a wonderful lot of players with access to the upper echelons of the game that they could not have achieved by any other route.

Of all of the sagas that feature has initiated, perhaps the most entertaining and significant is that developed by Lee Trevino.

It is a well known and oft told story of the triumph of guts, determination and wit that constitute the Lee Trevino saga. He came from a deprived background and without money or other means managed to find his way into golf, develop a unique golf game and battle his way through the Open qualifying in 1967.

And so it was that Lee Trevino turned up at Baltusrol in 1967 to play in the United States Open Championship. And play he did, shooting 283 and finishing fifth. He won $6,000, which was no small fortune to him at that time in his life.

While he blew a goodly part of that prize money on appropriate celebrating with his friends, he kept enough of it to finance his foray onto the PGA Tour, where he won more than enough additional money to finance his career in professional golf.

That experience in the Open at Baltusrol in 1967 proved to him that he could play at the highest level of the game and with anyone.

Given that proof and his character and his extraordinary talent, in retrospect it was no surprise that only a year later the world of golf was introduced to a new and fascinating star when he won the U.S. Open Championship at Oak Hill with four sensational rounds of 69, 68, 69, and 69.

Among Lee's many engaging characteristics is a well-developed sense of humor. As an example, I once enjoyed a delightfully engaging dinner with Lee and Tom Watson in the course of which Lee, with relish, told the following story:

His financial success had enabled him and his wife to acquire a handsome house in a relatively exclusive neighborhood. On a warm day Lee was out at the front of the property with his shirt off, trimming a hedge. A Cadillac, driven by a chauffeur, pulled up to the curb and a heavily bejeweled woman put her head out of a rear window and said to Lee "How much an hour do you charge?" Lee responded, "Well, we have not settled that yet, but I sleep with the lady who lives in this house!"

The game of golf has been wonderfully enriched by all that Lee with his inimitable style has brought to it. All of us hooked on golf have special reason therefore to be grateful to the U.S. Open for in a real sense providing us with Lee Trevino.

One of the fascinating features of this championship is how the players relate to the requirements the golf course poses. The set up is more demanding than any they confront during the rest of the year.

One distinguishing feature of the setup of Open courses is how effectively the mental side of the game is brought into play. The players uniformly have mastered the mechanics of getting the ball from the tee into the hole. Put them on a course with commodious fairways and yielding greens that are moderately paced and they will shoot lights out. The difficulty of the rough on Open courses plays a major role in the mental side of the players' performances. It is not so much the difficulty of getting out of it as it is the fear of getting into it that affects how they play. While normally they can drive the ball with laser-like accuracy, that fear affects them mentally so that they often back off using the driver, for which they pay a price. When they do use it, the fear factor makes swing mechanics much more difficult.

It is interesting to observe how the players handle returning scores that are substantially, in some cases embarrassingly, higher than is their norm.

Some of them simply and gracefully deal with the problem in the same spirit that Ben Hogan once dealt with a like problem at The Masters. Ben was at or near the apex of his career in a year when the 12th green at Augusta was brick hard so that balls were ricocheting off it in all directions. That green was topic A of the tournament. When Hogan came into the press building at the end of a round, the first question put to him was "Isn't the 12th hole impossible?" Ben considered that question thoughtfully and said, "No, not necessarily; it just seems to call for more skill than I have at the moment."

Other disappointed Open competitors, however, of whom there are a disturbing lot, are more inclined to find someone or something other than themselves to blame for the disappointing results they produce. The usual target is the United States Golf Association, which is said in effect to be responsible for the poor scores because of the course set up.

There are distinct elements of character involved, first in dealing with difficult conditions on the course, and then dealing off the course with reactions to having failed.

As a good—or bad—example, depending on your point of view, a number of players were volubly critical of the set up of Pebble Beach in the last round of the 1992 Open. A number of those same players, it should be noted, were complimentary about the course set up during the first three days of the Open. Benign, still, damp weather had softened and slowed down the greens, making the course a relative pussy cat. On Sunday, however, the weather became a real factor. Sun and wind dried out the greens and the wind put a premium on ball control and course management. It was the same course and the same set up, how could it have been otherwise, but the weather turned it into something quite different from what it had been. It was both surprising and disappointing to observe how few of the best players in the game could handle it.

Tom Kite, to his eternal credit, handled it sensationally and got the 100 ton gorilla off his back of never having won a major championship.

There are fundamental philosophical premises for the approach of the USGA to the set up of a course for an Open Championship. They can be simply stated in terms of what someone presuming to be golf's national champion ought to be able to do:

- He ought to be able to drive the ball reasonable distances and consistently into fairways approximately 30 yards wide;
- He ought to have to deal with an appropriate penalty for shots which stray from the fairway;
- He ought to hit an appropriate number of greens in one, two or three shots depending on the par of the hole;
- He ought to have to deal with an appropriate penalty when he misses a green;
- He ought to be able to hit shots with sufficient precision so that they will hold on firm greens;
- He ought to be concerned, when he hits a green, about where the ball comes to rest in relation to where the hole is located;
- He ought to be able to putt consistently on greens paced to test his skill with the putter;
  (With reference to this element, I had a revealing encounter with a couple of players at a site where I was responsible for the course set up. I met them early in the morning in the hall of a hotel and one of them said, "Boy, Sandy, you look tired," and the other said, "You would look tired too if you had been out there all night on your hands and knees waxing the greens!")
- And, finally, our national champion ought to be able to deal with adversity with the patience and perseverance it takes to be a true champion.

Those fundamental premises have consistently been the guideposts for the set up of Open courses. The test of time certainly has proven their validity.

When I was responsible for setting up Winged Foot for the Open Championship (1974), inordinately high scores fueled so much controversy that I was moved to remind anyone who might be listening that our objective in setting up Open courses is not to humiliate the best players in the game, but rather simply to identify who they are.

The Masters

Each spring in a lovely setting in Georgia that was once a nursery and is now a perfectly beautiful golf course one of the more important of all the rites of spring gives all born-again golfers a new lease on life. I refer, of course, to The Masters.

There are a host of distinctive features that make The Masters one of the more important events in the whole history of golf.

The central feature, of course, is Bobby Jones. In the history of the game there are a dozen or so players who qualify as having been great. Bobby Jones certainly is among them and may well have been the greatest of them all. There can be no doubt that he was the most engaging great player to have played this game and his manifest love of the game is wonderfully recorded in all that he wrote about it.

He created the course at Augusta National in collaboration with Alister MacKenzie so that the course was the creation of two geniuses.

There are a lot of features in that course that are reflective of the love affair Bobby Jones had with The Old Course at St. Andrews. It provides a glorious test of golf, especially for The Masters field who are suitably challenged by it every spring.

The course also reflects Bobby Jones' understanding of the aesthetic feature of the game of golf. He chose the nursery setting, because he could visualize a course there which would be both great and stunningly beautiful. That vision was spectacularly realized in what he then created.

He then proceeded to create The Masters as a celebration of the playing of the game he loved so profoundly.

What a marvelous creation all that was—and is—for the game of golf.

Every spring the game of golf is presented to the world in a perfectly beautiful setting on a course designed so that the intrinsic and extrinsic drama that golf can provide is beautifully exposed.

It would not be possible to exaggerate the intensity of the drama that The Masters develops virtually every year. One extraordinary factor in that drama is that, while the original design had the first and second nines as they are now played, Jones reversed the nines for the playing of the first Masters. After that first year, however, he reverted to the original plan so that all the drama that develops out of the design of what now are the last nine holes occurs at the end rather than at the beginning of the last day's play.

With Bobby Jones so involved in all of the features of its origins, The Masters developed virtually instant tradition. The traditions of beauty, style, drama, respect for the game and a pantheon of great champions have continued to identify The Masters as one of the most distinctive happenings in the whole spectrum of sport.

It is entirely fitting that one of the most inspirational performers in any medium that was Bobby Jones should have as a living memorial to his greatness a happening that is as inspirational as The Masters continues to be.

The PGA Championship

I continue to lament the decision of the PGA to abandon the match play format for its championship.

The game of golf essentially originated as a match play game. As the game evolved, match play has been its predominant format. Virtually all of the golf played everywhere in the world, excepting by professionals and would-be professionals, is played at match play.

Match play has the element of personal combat, with two people having to deal with the game, the course and each other such that for one of them, so to speak, there will be no tomorrow.

That element gives this format some personality that is lacking in stroke play.

It also imposes on the player the necessity to meet the immediate challenge of at least matching his opponent's performance. If, for example, your opponent has holed his putt for a birdie, in dealing with your putt, also for a birdie, it simply is not an acceptable result to miss it, whereas, in stroke play, scoring par on the hole would be acceptable.

Let's suppose you have hit a long but wayward tee shot. If your opponent has played a spectacular shot and put his ball on the green with a makeable putt, in match play you have no sensible choice but to go for it, whereas in stroke play, the prudent play might be to lay up, hoping to get up and down with a chip and a putt.

There also is the redeeming feature in match play that if you grievously foul up a hole you lose only one hole, whereas in stroke play you may have foreclosed a tolerable result.

The PGA Championship evolved as a match play event reflecting all these factors. Over the 42 years it was played at this format it produced a sensational series of chapters in the history of the game.

One of the more interesting of those chapters was the David vs. Goliath encounter in the PGA final of 1938 when Paul Runyan played Sam Snead. Paul, who is a small man, was a remarkably short hitter, while Snead with his size and athletic ability hit the ball prodigious distances with extraordinary consistency. The match was a 36-hole match, with the essential pattern established early on. Runyan would be playing first to the green on every four- or five-par hole, often on the four pars with a wood, whereas Snead had just a short iron. That, as it turned out, produced an insurmountable problem for Sam, because Paul was playing his shots into the green so spectacularly well that virtually every time Sam sized up his shot to the green he was looking at Paul's ball lying disturbingly close to the hole. To say that Sam could not handle that recurring image is to be charitable. Once again David clobbered Goliath, this time by 8 and 7.

In 1941 at Cherry Hills I was privileged to spectate a PGA Championship 36-hole match between Byron Nelson and Ben Hogan, and what a match it was. The contrast in personalities and styles added much flavor. Each matched the spectacular shots the other was hitting and battled so brilliantly right down to the last green, where Nelson won 2-and-1. What a break for me to have witnessed those two giants going head to head over 36 holes and each displaying so much of what it takes to be a great player.

One measure of how much inherent drama there can be in match play is suggested by two players in a stroke play event having left the rest of the field far behind and, being paired together, generating excitement from having, in effect, match play. The classic confrontation of Watson vs. Nicklaus in the British Open at Turnberry in 1977 provides such an example.

When the PGA Championship succumbed in 1958 to the siren allure of more television money, the game lost a great championship and the world of golf was deprived of the matchless fascination of watching the greatest players in the game going head-to-head, when for one of them there is no tomorrow.

To lament such a loss is not an adequate response; it calls at least for a cry of anguish.

The Ryder Cup Team
and the President
of the United States

An incident which developed around a recent Ryder Cup Match deserves some commentary. Bill Clinton, President of the United States, invited the members of the 1993 U.S. Team to visit him in the White House before taking off for England. Some of the responses to that invitation were distressing.

Some team members expressed outrage at alleged confiscatory taxes and references to Vietnam draft dodging. Even non-team member Greg Norman apparently got into the act, being quoted to the effect that he would not want to be a guest of someone who had imposed a retroactive tax on him! I somehow could not generate any sympathy for Greg's lament over having to come up with a relatively minuscule piece of his income to help deal with the deficit. In any event, I thought and think all such commentary missed the point of the White House invitation by light years, and was just plain dumb.

The point, of course, is that the office of the President of The United States, and not whoever may be its current occupant, gives the invitation the special dignity and significance it deserves. The institution of the Presidency has served this country effectively, notwithstanding whatever may be the judgments we have on those who pass through the office.

It was not surprising, it was rather perfectly predictable, that Tom Watson would have the right perspective in pointing out that it was the institution—the office of the President of The United States—that certainly deserved appropriate respect.

That bit of nonsense on the part of some of the professional golfers on this Ryder Cup Team provoked some additional musing about how far from the real world successful touring professionals live and how their being so insulated from reality could help explain, but certainly not excuse, the flawed judgments discussed above.

For the ordinary mortal, it is almost impossible to imagine what the oasis life of the successful touring professional is like. His golf skills give him a very special status that includes being the object of envy, admiration and adulation by masses of people, including very important and successful people in industry, commerce, finance and politics. The adulation of those sorts of people gets expressed, for example, in lining up to pay a lot of money for the privilege of playing a round of golf with the professional (and a lot more if the outing includes being able to socialize with him over cocktails and dinner). The professional is also courted by a dazzling array of entrepreneurs vying to add considerably to his wealth through promotions and projects. He also is catered to by sponsors of golf tournaments who see to it that his every need, from luxurious courtesy cars to baby-sitters, is more than comfortably accommodated from the moment he arrives in the sponsor's city. I once noted to a professional with whom I was playing in a pro-am that the logical next step would be for sponsors to provide sedan chairs and eunuchs with palm fronds to provide comfortable transportation to the players between shots.

And then the professional performs at places like Augusta National in The Masters where, as he approaches virtually every green, he is accorded a hero's welcome—something like General deGaulle received when he led the march into liberated Paris.

Now, I do not want to be misunderstood as being critical of the professional golfers for being the objects of all this unreal attention and adulation. They are not responsible for how people relate to their skills.

While I am sympathetic to how difficult living in that world makes it for people to see themselves and the real world with any sensible sense of perspective, I think that status imposes a special responsibility to get and stay in touch with reality. When the President of the United States offers to honor them and the game they play, they should recognize the invitation as an honor and a privilege.

The Ryder Cup
and the Belfry

As The Ryder Cup Match becomes increasingly important, I wonder about the selection of the venue for the playing of the match in Britain. When you consider all of the sensational links courses that so distinguish the game in that part of the world, and indeed tie the playing of the game to its origins, it is puzzling, to say the least, that the venue selectors would select a course in the English Midlands which looks like it was transplanted from a resort in Florida.

I do not mean to demean Florida resort courses, although I must say that the style of architecture reflected in so many of them does not appeal to me. I simply mean that the links game available on those classic links courses is a much superior form of golf, particularly for a great occasion.

There are so many features that distinguiksh the links game. The necessity to calculate bounce and roll in the playing of the shot; the requirements of dealing with the elements, particularly the winds, that have such an important part in the playing of those courses; the self-management required in at least occasionally dealing with bad bounces and awkward lies; the fescue turf grass on those firm fairways that adds so much satisfaction to a crisply struck iron shot; the golf aesthetics that so stimulate the player as he views the course from the first tee and continues to stimulate him as the aesthetics of the course are revealed to him in the course of the playing of a round.

None of these distinguishing features is available at The Belfry. What you see there are lush, green fairways, yielding greens, holes dug in the ground and filled with water to create artificial hazards, and a course on which the game is played from point to point in the air.

I am moved to add that the visage of a water fountain playing in the middle of an artificial lake fronting the 18th green violates my sensibilities. Fountains belong in civic plazas and parks, and formal gardens. Wherever else you might consider putting them, they seem to me to be singularly out of place in the United Kingdom where old Tom Morris worked his ball under the winds on the classic links and the spirit of Shivas Irons should pervade the atmosphere.

History and tradition, moreover, are such vital parts of the golf mystique. The classic links courses on that island are loaded with history and tradition, characteristics that are singularly missing at The Belfry.

Why should it matter that the venue selectors choose a Florida-style golf course in the English Midlands for this Match? The great occasions—and this Match certainly has become one of them—are showcases for the game. A vital form of the game, namely links golf, deserves all of the showcasing that it can get.

In view of the obvious attractions and the multiple reasons for siting this match at one of the classic links courses in the United Kingdom, you have to wonder why the site selectors selected The Belfry. There is an aroma of commercial interests being served. It may be unrealistic to think that commercial interests should be subordinated to the good of the game, but I fervently do so think and harbor the hope, therefore, that The Belfry will be reserved for those who want to play Florida-style golf in the English Midlands and that the Match over there be restored to the links where the game began and true game is still available to be played.

The Ryder Cup and the Right Spirit

As I watched the television coverage of The 1993 Ryder Cup Match, I especially enjoyed the camera coverage of Tom Watson relating to the event, his team and their triumphs. A lot of Tom's personality and character were manifested in that coverage. The viewer was accorded some interesting insights into how Tom relates to the game and to the people who play it.

From my point of view, there was an accomplishment realized in this Match far more important than the triumph of Tom's team. There was a revival, or perhaps more accurately a restoration, of the right spirit that pervaded the atmosphere of this Match. It was first manifested in the relationship of the players with their teammates and then was apparent in the sportsmanship that characterized the relationships between the two teams. Finally, and perhaps most importantly, it was reflected in the collective attitude of the galleries in displaying an appropriate degree of partisanship while appreciating the quality of golf they were privileged to witness played with the sportsmanship that so impressively distinguishes the game of golf.

There was a dramatic difference between that total atmosphere and that which so afflicted the 1991 Match.

The most important winner of the 1993 Ryder Cup Match, therefore, was the game of golf!

There can be no doubt than Tom Watson made a major contribution to that triumph.

A couple of weeks before he took his team to the United Kingdom, Tom telephoned me to discuss a letter I had written to him expressing concerns about the atmosphere of tension building around the Ryder Cup Match. Tom clearly shared those concerns and expressed his determination to do everything he could, using the leverage of his captaincy and the credibility he enjoys—and richly deserves—to diffuse those tensions and develop the spirit of sportsmanship that should characterize the playing of this Match. He discussed in some depth with me how he proposed to do what he could to achieve that result. He deserves a full measure of gratitude from all of us hooked on golf for then proceeding to do so much that matters so much.

The Ping Lawsuit

One of the more disturbing developments afflicting sports in recent years has been resort to lawsuits to settle differences. A case in point is litigation that has been a serious threat to the structure of the governance of the game of golf. The case involved Karsten Manufacturing Company, the creator of Ping clubs, and the PGA Tour.

The case evolved out of the esoteric subject of the shape of grooves in the faces of iron clubs. Notwithstanding the Rule of Golf made by the United States Golf Association that the grooves could be V, U or square in cross section, the Tour attempted to impose a rule for Tour play that confined groove shape to the V configuration.

One effect of such a Tour rule would have been to prevent players with Ping clubs from using those clubs on the Tour, because those clubs have U-shaped grooves.

Karsten filed suit against the Tour in Federal District Court in Phoenix seeking to enjoin the Tour from invoking the Tour grooves rule and alleging serious money damages. The controversy took a terrible turn for the worse when the Tour filed what amounted to a counter suit in Florida alleging that during a period about 20 years ago, Karsten had fraudulently produced clubs that violated the then USGA grooves rule so as to give players using those clubs an illegal advantage.

Many millions of dollars in legal fees and heaven knows how much time, energy and emotion were consumed over a period of years by those lawsuits. Deane Beman, then the Tour's Commissioner, developed diverticulitis, which must have been at least part of the price he paid for his personal involvement.

In the pretrial skirmishing, the Tour lost virtually every battle, including suffering a preliminary injunction preventing the Tour from invoking the Tour rule pending the outcome of the litigation.

Finally, shortly before the case was to be tried in Phoenix, reason prevailed and a settlement was reached. The Tour abandoned its fraud claims and the Florida case was dismissed. The Tour abandoned the Tour grooves rule and confirmed that clubs with grooves conforming to the USGA rules would be usable on the Tour. The Tour confirmed the United States Golf Association as the governing body of gof in this country and agreed to deviate from USGA rules only if an independent blue-ribbon commission found some significant commercial necessity for the Tour to do so. And the Tour agreed to pay Karsten a lot of money, the amount of which has not been announced but is believed to be many millions of dollars.

While this result certainly was a triumph for Karsten, it left a core principle at least somewhat in limbo. That principle, which was at the core of this litigation, was whether there would be two games played in this country, one played on the Tour and another played by the rest of us and whether there would be just one governing body, that is the United States Golf Association acting without any conflicts of interest solely with regard to the best interests of the whole game of golf.

The so-called blue-ribbon commission intrudes another body into that structure. If that commission were to act so that the Tour is playing a different game from the rest of us, Karsten's victory will have become a defeat for the game of golf.

Ball Too Far

Historically there have been a number of rules adopted to limit the distance the ball could be hit. The most recent of these was the adoption of the Overall Distance Standard in the mid-70s. Nonetheless, I and some others, most notably including Bill Campbell, continue to be concerned that this factor in the game is out of control and that the resulting problem needs to be dealt with.

At a 1996 meeting of the USGA's Implements and Ball Committee I was invited to express my concern. I did so as follows:

The analysis has to start with one of two threshold questions. Is there a serious problem? I certainly think there is a problem, and I think that it is so serious as to threaten fundamentally and detrimentally to change the game.

That thought leads to a question of how we define the game in this setting. I think the game is defined by the skills required to play it according to the standards set by the play of the game's premier players. We should want to maintain one game with one set of standards against which each of us individually can measure our respective performances rather than establishing several different games.

What then is the problem? As I see it, the ball is being hit too far. The distance factor is out of balance with the other skills that should be required to play the game.

Having said that I note that there is an absolute correlation at all levels of the game between distance and scoring. It certainly should be no surprise to have confirmed that the farther you can hit it within reasonable bounds the easier the game becomes.

There are statistical arguments to the effect that nothing is developing in this distance area that should be the cause for any concern. My evaluation of that argument in sum is as follows:

- Most statistics simply do not tell the whole story and are, in this setting, misleading. To the extent that they deal with averages, they do not tell you what clubs were used or how far the ball was being hit at the upper end of the scale of distances that created the average. They also are affected by particular conditions in which the statistics were developed. For example, a couple of years ago at the AT&T one of the holes at Poppy Hills being used to develop driving distance statistics for the Tour was so structured that 240 yards was a very big hit.

- Scoring statistics (i.e., those indicating that scoring has not been affected) are affected by extraordinarily difficult conditions such as those that ballooned the scores at Pebble Beach in 1992 and those (i.e. firmer faster greens) that are increasingly a factor in The Masters. When you consider how much more difficult U.S. Tour courses have become in the last 20 years with narrowed fairways, more and more difficult rough and firmer, faster greens, winning score reduction of four shots per event strikes me as evidence that the distance factor indeed is having a significant effect.

- Most statistics simply do not square with the realities being experienced and observed in the playing of the game. Those realities include…

- Our own observations and experiences in the playing of the game, and the observations of others who are concerned that the ball in fact is being hit too far.

- The observations of people who make their living designing golf courses. They are moving turning points (i.e., the point from which they anticipate second shots on the hole will be played). Turning points have moved from 250 yards from the tee to 265 yards and now in many cases to 275 yards. Those people responsible for creating golf courses are simply responding to what they know is happening in the playing of the game.

- The 15th hole at Augusta as it is played in The Masters surely provides a most useful clinic for the evaluation of this question. Gene Sarazen made his double eagle with a 4-wood. With the hole playing some 40 yards longer, Tiger Woods (who may be a tiger but he certainly is no gorilla) on a damp still day hit it over the green with a 9-iron! To those, if there are any, who are inclined to dismiss Tiger in this setting simply as a phenom, I say that he is at least a harbinger and in any event, all of the other players hitting that green with medium irons certainly cannot be dismissed.

- It now develops that Jack Nicklaus, when he was hitting the ball awe-inspiring distances, was a harbinger, because a whole host of players are now hitting the ball as far as he did in his prime.

- Surely no one can seriously question the fact that the character of the game has been fundamentally changed. That is a one iron that Ben Hogan is pictured hitting onto the four-par 18th green at Merion. You now very seldom see anything more than a 5-iron used on a second shot on any hole other than a par five. Par fives of over 500 yards are routinely hit in two usually with an iron club. On the Senior Tour as well, 500-yard par fives are almost routinely played in two shots to the green.

While someone might want to dismiss John Daly as some sort of an aberration, I cannot discount how he emasculated and reduced the requirements for playing The Old Course in the British Open simply by neutralizing the hazards on that course with the distance he was driving the ball.

Those who conclude that there currently is no problem of real substance have to answer the second threshold question; and that is, is there sufficient possibility that such a problem will develop in the foreseeable future so that those responsible for the preservation of the game ought to be considering how to deal with it? I resist belaboring the point by simply observing that there is no reasonable premise for assuming that such a problem will not develop in the foreseeable future. No one can sensibly assume that golf somehow will be immune from that which has so affected other games, that is, attracting in increasing numbers stronger, better conditioned athletes.

Accepting the premise that there is a problem, either currently or in prospect, the question becomes what is the source of the problem.

Is it the ball? I agree with Frank Hannigan (i.e., his article in a February, 2001 issue of *Golf Digest*). While I can wish that we who adopted it had not allowed the innovation tolerance in the Overall Distance Standard ("ODS"), I am satisfied that that standard effectively put a cap on how much ball design and construction could add to distance. So while the ball has contributed something to the problem, that contribution has been capped. (Since this was written in 1996 technology has found a way with a combination, as I understand it, of launch angle and spin rate to create a ball that conforms to the ODS but, with optimum conditions, goes considerably farther with a given amount of energy input.)

Some history of the adoption of ODS is pertinent here. It was a manifestation of concern 20 plus years ago that the ball was being hit too far. That concern was intensified when Acushnet produced a new Titleist with aerodynamic characteristics that added to the lift factor and caused the ball to fly farther. The Executive Committee asked USGA technical director Frank Thomas to come up with an empirical solution that would cap what ball design and construction could contribute to distance. He did so. To avoid a new standard outlawing existing balls, the standard was set to accommodate the longest ball. When test and innovative tolerances were added, the standard was extended to 296 yards! I thought then that such a standard distance was out of bounds, but took comfort from the thought that having created the cap, we were in a position sensibly to roll it back.

For some 20 years I have been advocating (some might call it agitating) that the process of when and how to effect the roll back get started. In the meantime, as I see it, the problem has been exacerbated.

Is equipment the source of the problem? I think that much of what is being made of mystical elements and exotic materials in the equipment category is a lot of nonsense. I do understand, however, that properly designed equipment utilizing materials that are now available and are effectively fitted to what I would call the swing metabolism of the individual player certainly can contribute to what is the ultimate source of the problem.

While course conditions (e.g. firmer, closer cut fairways) add to the problem, the ultimate source simply is clubhead speed. There are two absolutes in this setting. One is that E does indeed equal MC^2. The other is that the C factor, i.e., clubhead speed, is the one factor in this whole setting that we cannot control. I cannot imagine how anyone who is comfortable with the current situation could also be comfortable with the assumption that there will not be an increasing number of stronger, better coordinated players with equipment more suitable to their respective swing metabolisms who will consistently be putting the ball into orbit.

Does the problem pose a serious threat to the game? I cannot think how anyone could conclude that it does not. I think the analogy to what has developed in tennis is specially apt. In tennis, the combination of better coordinated, stronger, athletes playing with equipment developed so as to emphasize the effects of their strengths increased the speed of service balls by some 25%. The result has been to materially change the game to its detriment by reducing the combination of skills required to play it and over-emphasize the effect of power. I think it is clear that golf is facing a threat with those same elements.

Golf's playing fields are finite. Suitable sites for golf courses, near population centers are even more finite. Unless the problem is corralled, new courses will have to be 7,500 yards long and grow longer, old courses will be obsolete (witness the current threat to

Merion) and the competitive advantage enjoyed by the power hitter will be out of sight.

That leads to consideration of what is the solution. While the ball is not the problem (as I thought in 1996), it does (in any event) provide the solution. The solution is to change the ball specifications (e.g. initial velocity) so that the game is kept within bounds. By such a simple statement, I do not mean to imply that getting the right set of specifications will be simple. On the other hand, it also will not be impossible.

There certainly are elements of legal and practical problems in achieving the solution.

I must say, that the governing bodies cannot allow themselves to be distracted and much less paralyzed by legal concerns. I should also say that, for whatever my judgment may be worth, properly handled, dealing with this problem has zero legal exposure.

Practical considerations pose more of a problem.

Obviously the R&A independently has to come to like conclusions.

Another major constituency is the Tour. If the Tour and the manufacturers got together in opposition to any change in the status quo, the cause could be lost.

There also is the possibility that this problem, one way or another, could spawn a so-called "Tour ball."

If those responsible for the preservation of the game are dissuaded from acting because they conclude that the problem is too tough to handle, they are abdicating control of the game to the Tour and the manufacturers. I have to say with what I trust all concerned would recognize as due respect, that combination would be the ultimate in commercial interests conflicting with objective control of the game.

Then there are regional associations and last, but in a real sense foremost, the millions of people who play the game and look to the governing bodies for the leadership required to preserve it.

It deserves further emphasis that governing bodies cannot afford to be distracted, much less paralyzed, by the practical problems.

What all this adds up to is a historic crossroads in the history and development of the game. It certainly calls for all of the foresight and leadership that can be brought to bear.

I further note that creative handling of this problem could eventually lead to one ball for the game. What a perfectly wonderful development that would be.

I need at least to pause to expand a bit on that thought. When the suggested local "one ball" rule was adopted, a small step in the right direction was taken. The governing bodies need to keep going. Selecting specific balls for specific course conditions (e.g. low trajectory balls if the wind is blowing, two piece hard cover if fairways are firm and the greens are soft, and wound balata balls when the fairways and greens are firm) is a contradiction of the one-game premise.

Furthermore, in designing specifications for the one ball, the solutions to the distance problem as well as the problem of the ball holding, or staying close to, the line when it should be hooking and slicing could be neatly packaged.

By advocating one ball, I do not mean to suggest selecting one manufacturer to make a given ball. I rather mean developing the specifications that define a ball which every manufacturer would be entitled to make. All of us, therefore, in all conditions would indeed be playing the same game.

Finally, I need to repeat that ever since the Overall Distance Standard was adopted 21 years ago I have been advocating consideration of what to do about the fact or at least the prospect of the ball being hit too far. I have not been able to accumulate much of an audience in those 21 years. It is most gratifying, therefore, to have been accorded the privilege of addressing this audience.

While, since I wrote and presented the foregoing to the Implements & Ball committee of the USGA (attended by representatives of the R&A) the ball has added significantly to the problem, that development only adds conviction to my view that the above suggested approach is the right, if not the only, way to deal with the problem.

Since the foregoing memo was written five years ago, subsequent developments have added emphasis and urgency to the validity of the thrust of that memo. When Tiger Woods on Master Sunday 2001 reduced the 18th hole to a drive and short sand wedge it was a dramatically emphatic answer to the abiding questions of whether there is or will be a problem.

That tee shot, plus many others by several players on several holes during that Masters, convinced Hootie Johnson, Augusta National's President, that there is a problem, illustrated by having substantial four pars reduced to drive and wedge holes. Hootie decided to deal with it by adding substantial length to several holes on that classic course.

Hootie's response was understandable, because as the Rules now stand, he only had two options. One would be to add tough rough and narrow the landing areas. What was done at Carnoustie in the 1999 British Open illustrates how counterproductive such a solution is. His other option, i.e. to add considerable length to the holes, while perhaps the better of bad choices only exacerbates the problem by putting more emphasis on power and making the holes more difficult for the shorter hitters.

The decision-makers, therefore, need to give Hootie, and everyone else trying to preserve the design values and characteristics of their golf courses, a better, in fact the only tenable, choice. They need to develop ball specifications that will restore reasonable balance between shotmaking and power and will preserve those values and characteristics.

One Ball

Having so referred to the one-ball concept, I expanded on that thought with a subsequent memorandum to the USGA's Implements and Ball Committee expressing the following point of view:

The term one ball means that the Rules of Golf specify ball characteristics so that all balls with which the game is played have fundamentally the same playing characteristics.

As the rules now stand, there are several specifications in effect identifying characteristics that all balls must have. The one ball concept simply requires adding to those specifications so that the desired result is achieved.

One way of thinking about the concept is to ask a material question or two. If the game of golf did not exist and were being invented, would the inventor include one ball in the definition of the game? If the answer is no, then the question becomes how far would the inventor go in specifying common characteristics for golf balls and why would the inventor stop there?

If the answer is yes, then the question becomes why not proceed to add to the specifications in the rules so as to define one ball to be played by those who play golf. Analysis of that question has several elements.

Would there be legal challenges? The possibilities range from quite likely to absolutely. Should legal challenges deter the decision makers? Aside from making sure that the required process is observed, the answer is absolutely not.

Do legal challenges pose a risk to the financial viability of the

USGA? The answer is "absolutely not" for two reasons. One is that it is most likely that the USGA would prevail. The other is that a preemptive declaratory relief action taken by the USGA prior to implementing the decision would determine any possible legal question and, in the unlikely event that the USGA were to lose, it simply would not implement the decision.

Is the one-ball concept technically feasible? The answer is absolutely.

Are there practical problems to consider? There most certainly are and they pose the real threat that such an eminently sound idea could not, as a practical matter, be implemented.

Obviously, it would be fatally impractical for the USGA to proceed to implement such a rules change without having the support of its constituency.

Obviously, the R&A would have to be persuaded. That could be difficult, but not impossible.

Would the U.S. and European and other Tours be persuaded? Not likely, given the economic factors involved but, I submit, not impossible. If the U.S. Tour were to be persuaded it is reasonable to expect that the others would follow. Persuading the U.S. Tour has two factors going for it, primarily that the concept of having one game where the import of equipment is reduced and the import of skill is increased is eminently sound and there has been some at least fairly serious consideration given to a so-called "tour ball." Here again, patience, perseverance and proper persuasiveness could carry the day.

The manufacturers. For obvious reasons it is, to put it mildly, unlikely that the manufacturers could be persuaded. On the other hand, the total market for golf balls would not be affected so that, taken collectively, they would have no legitimate complaint that realization of the objective creates a money loser for them.

The general golfing public. The ultimate reaction from this vital constituency would depend on two elements: 1) the persuasiveness of the reasons for adopting the one ball rule; 2) and how much difference, if any, the playing of that ball would make in their over-all enjoyment of the game.

The process. The first step should be strictly analytical. The threshold question should be: does the almost infinite variety of playing characteristics of balls conforming to the existing Rules affect the skill factor in the playing of the game and if so, how and how much? A couple of examples serve as illustrations. One relates to course conditions. If the course is wet and the greens are soft, presumably the player will gain some advantage by playing with a ball which provides less spin. If, on the other hand, the course is dry and the greens are firm, presumably the player will gain some advantage by playing with a ball that provides him with more spin. The other example relates to the wind factor. A player playing in windy conditions presumably would gain some advantage by playing a low trajectory ball into the wind and a high trajectory ball downwind.

Such examples as those caused the development of the "one ball" local rule. This rule, which committees governing events are authorized to adopt, provides that during play of a round, the balls a player uses must be of the same brand and type. For example, if a player starts a round playing a Titleist 90 compression balata, balls of that brand and type are the only balls he may use during the course of the round. That rule, which committees adopt for all USGA events, all Tour events, and a large portion of events conducted by regional golf associations, was created in response to players using several balls with differing playing characteristics in the course of a round depending on the particular conditions (e.g., wind, green firmness, etc.) prevailing on a particular hole.

The principle that was the genesis for that local rule is the same as that promoting one ball for the game. At least analytically, it would seem to be a relatively small step from that rule to a rule which says everyone playing the game plays with a ball which has the same fundamental playing characteristics.

It should be noted that the foregoing does not consider what characteristics the one ball should have. That process should be no more difficult than the processes that led to the establishment of the current specifications, each of which affects the playing characteristics of the ball.

Since writing this memorandum some years ago, I have not changed the views expressed in it. They may not be practical, but they certainly are irrefutably right! Whatever may be the practical obstacles, I persist in the hope that what is irrefutably right can overcome them.

Golf Course
Architecture

Access to the Game

Two related factors limit the numbers of people who can gain access to the game. One is the cost involved. The other is lack of facilities for people of modest (or less) means to learn and to play.

When you consider how much playing the game can add to peoples' lives, doing something effective to deal with those factors has real import. Furthermore, there is a sociological plus to be gained from doing so. People who work with young people in an effort to direct them to constructive rather than destructive activity affirm how effective involving them in golf can be.

There are some programs which are working. An excellent example is that created in Tennessee by a joint venture of the Tennessee Golf Association and the Tennessee PGA.

However commendable and useful such programs are, much more can and should be done.

What is needed is a nation wide project mobilizing the resources of the golf community. I visualize such a project as being put together and energized by the USGA and involving the other constituents of the golf community such as the PGA of America, the PGA Tour, ball and equipment manufacturers and golf publications.

While those other constituents should be motivated by how much good could come from such a project, their profit motives should be satisfied by the economic benefits for each of them from substantially increasing the numbers of people playing the game.

The structure for the project should be a separate non-profit corporation funded by the participants and staffed to make it work.

That corporation would promote, organize and provide financing which would:

- attract people to playing the game;
- providing them with:
  — equipment;
  — education about the values and etiquette of the game;
  — instruction; and
  — facilities for practice and playing.

Municipalities should be a prime resource for providing affordable facilities. Municipalities should be motivated to do so by all the communal benefits that would flow from such facilities. Municipalities can make land available. The facilities could be economically financed by revenue bonds providing tax advantages. The non-profit corporation could provide the collateral guarantees for such bonds which would make the project economically viable.

The facilities could be designed and constructed to provide affordable golf for a wonderful lot of people.

Is such a project feasible? I have no doubt that it is. As golf becomes a booming industry, the financial resources should be available. All it then takes is the will, wit, commitment and leadership to make it happen.

The foregoing was written before the PGA Tour with significant support from the USGA initiated the First Tee Project. The foregoing coincidentally, provides an almost precise blueprint of that program.

The program is up and running, and provides wonderful promise for attracting to the game and making golf accessible for many thousands of young people throughout the country whose lives will be enhanced, indeed in many cases transformed.

Restoring Pebble Beach

The United States Open Championship was coming to Pebble Beach in 1972. That was the impetus for a phone call in 1968 from the then-president of The Del Monte Properties Company that owned and operated Pebble Beach. He asked if I would take on a project of restoring the course and doing whatever else should be done to have it ready for the Open. For me that was akin to being asked to restore a great work of art which had suffered some deterioration.

Like a remarkable number of great courses (e.g., Oakmont, Pine Valley, The Chicago Golf Club) Pebble Beach had been designed by two amateur golfers. One, Douglas Grant, had died, but the other, Jack Neville, was living a reclusive life in the nearby city of Pacific Grove. He was pleased to accept my proposal that he join me in the project.

After a detailed survey of the course we decided that it needed the following:

- a sand bunker restored at the left front of the first green;
- more length for the second hole by moving the tee back as far as we could;
- lengthening the 3rd hole by moving the tee back;
- adding a pot bunker and restructuring the existing bunker in the drive zone on 4;
- rebuilding and moving the 5th tee;
- enlarging the drive zone fairway bunker on 6 and redesigning the bunker affecting the second shot;
- adding bunkers in the drive zone on the left side of 9;
- adding length to the 10th hole by moving the tee back and redesigning the bunkering in the drive zone that had original-

ly been designed for a tee located on the right side of the 9th green;

- redesigning the bunker in the drive zone on 16 to enlarge and deepen it. (It was into this bunker that Tom Watson hit his tee shot in the last round of the 1982 Open and cost him his then one-shot lead over Nicklaus. He restored that lead with the chip from the rough on 17 which went squarely into the hole.)

It was gratifying to be so involved with that masterpiece, most especially in collaboration with the man whose vision created the original design. That involvement confirmed my judgment, developed when I first played the course in 1936, that Pebble Beach is unique.

The prime premise for that judgment is the routing devised by Messrs. Grant and Neville. That routing simply provides the most effective use possible for the God-given site: two inland holes, the 3rd providing a glimpse of Carmel Bay, followed by 4 running alongside beautiful Stillwater Cove. Five then was a totally inland hole. All of which sets up the stunning experience of walking onto the 6th tee and being presented with a panorama of Carmel Bay and the coastline and ocean beyond. From there the course provides vistas and challenges that stir more than the senses; they engage the soul of the golfer.

It certainly was specially suitable that this was the setting in 1972 in which the premier player of all time, Jack Nicklaus, won the United States Open Championship.

Spanish Bay
and Some Notes
on Golf Course
Architecture

The experience with Pebble Beach followed a like experience with the San Francisco Golf Club and subsequent involvement in restoring a part of the 8th green at Cypress Point that had been removed when Robert Trent Jones Sr. redesigned that green around 1950. Another dimension of involvement with course design was added in the mid to late 1980s collaborating with Robert Trent Jones Jr. and Tom Watson in the design of The Links At Spanish Bay on the Monterey Peninsula. Other design work has developed working with Jim Summers, an extraordinarily talented designer, on four courses in California, and collaborating with Mike Poellot and Tom Fazio on another course on the Monterey Peninsula.

While law practice has remained my primary occupation, which I have found very satisfying, there are extraordinary stimuli derived from designing a golf course. You are engaged in an act of sculpture. The landscape is your medium. Your object is to create a work of art which will have all the aesthetic quality you can give it and that will be a permanent resource for quality experiences for countless people.

Being involved in such an enterprise with two such distinctive personalities as Robert Trent Jones Jr. and Tom Watson was specially engaging. In addition to working harmoniously together, we had some unusual challenges. The property had been a beautiful piece of links land which had been mined out to bedrock so that the high silica content sand could be sold. To restore its links look and character required a lot of creativity.

The challenge was to persuade the owners to permit us to design a links course. It took considerable persuasiveness on our part and even more courage on theirs to achieve the desired result. Our most persuasive point was that the owners would then have three courses on the Monterey Peninsula, Pebble Beach, Spyglass Hill and Spanish Bay, each with distinctly different character and each providing a distinctly different experience in the playing of the game.

The three of us were also persuaded that the links game deserved to have a place on this continent, and we had a virtually perfect setting in which to provide it.

We then had to persuade the California Coastal Commission. There are not enough pages to begin to describe how difficult that was. Two factors should provide some clue. There were six staff people and 12 commissioners concerned with the project. Not one of those 18 people played golf. At our first public hearing one of the commissioners stated that golf was the silliest game ever created and he could not be persuaded that one square centimeter of the earth's surface should be set aside for the playing of such an absurd game.

In the end, however, patience, perseverance and persuasiveness carried the day and Tom, Bob and I were permitted to realize our plan to create a links course.

The plan provided for restoring as nearly as we could the rolling dunes that had existed before the property was mined out. Some useable material was located in the forest a mile or so away and a conveyor belt was constructed to transport the material to the site.

Using that material, we sculpted the landscape and laid out a links course in it.

Tom Watson established the theme of our project in a promotional video shot before we started construction. He was seated on a log on one of the few remnant dunes. After a short comment on our objective he looked into the camera and said, "When we finish, you will practically be able to hear the bagpipes play!"

Indeed a piper does play there at sundown each day—part of the resort's way of reminding guests of the special landscape around the hotel. As I return to the site in the early evening and see that piper, silhouetted against the evening sky producing the oddly soulful sounds from the pipes, I am thrilled with the thought that we did indeed create a course that links the game to its Scottish origins.

Golf course architecture is a subject which engages virtually everyone who plays the game. That engagement extends beyond being critics. We are all putative architects. Having been privileged to participate in restoring and creating golf courses, I have been able to attempt to translate concepts into applications.

All this has stimulated development of a number of points of view.

They start with an aphorism attributed to Jimmy Demaret: "Golf and sex are the only two activities a man can thoroughly enjoy without being able to do them very well."

That aphorism poses the primary question for the architect, namely for whose enjoyment is the course being designed?

That question leads to consideration of the proliferation of courses being designed by players whose careers have been confined to playing stroke play golf for prize money. I believe those designers have two obstacles to overcome in reaching a right result. The first is a tendency to design courses which their peers will enjoy without regard for the rest of us. The second obstacle is that their experience with the game has been so intensely focused on the elements of their own extraordinary skills that they have difficulty relating their designs to the skills of ordinary players.

I do not mean to assert or imply that those players cannot produce courses which meet the ultimate test, which is to provide stimulating manageable challenges for the broadest possible spectrum of abilities. I do believe, however, that a number of their courses fail that test.

Providing challenges for a spectrum of players is the hallmark of a great architect. Designing a course that can only be sensibly played by premier players is as simple as designing one that poses few challenges for anyone. The artistry of the great architects is expressed in designs which provide stimulating challenges for the premier player and quality experiences for virtually all of the rest of us.

One element of effective design is to sensibly limit the number of forced carries and provide alternate routes for those who cannot handle them. Related to that element is provision of access to the greens. I do not mean that every green must be reachable by a shot which rolls onto it. That characteristic, however, should be the prevalent characteristic. Such provision enables the better players to have the option of flying the ball to the green or bouncing it on. This option enables the weaker players, especially women, to get to the green instead of being required to play a shot beyond their abilities. Obviously, the importance of that characteristic increases on courses where wind is a prevalent factor.

The importance of being able to play a good deal of the course with shots that bounce and roll relates to another useful characteristic, namely providing the element of chance in the design. The paucity of the element of chance in the design of our courses reflects a prevalent difference between the playing of the game in this country and in Britain. Here we play largely an airborne game where the ball stops very near the point where it hits. Over there, a large part of the game is played on the ground, the player being called upon to calculate a good deal of bounce and roll in working out his shots. My bias is for their game, and I wish there were more of it available to play in this country. Whichever game you prefer, however, I submit that it would be more interesting and more exciting if some element of chance were either left in or built into it by design.

That thought in turn leads to comment on the proliferation of the island green. The 17th hole of the Tournament Players course in Florida has spawned an awful number of progeny. While those sorts of holes can provide stimulating challenges for the accomplished player, they have a torture-chamber impact on the ordinary player. As they proliferate, it is no surprise that one course has even expanded the concept of the stationary island green with a green that floats with a motor on it to provide a target that changes daily—the 14th hole at Coeur d'Alene Resort, Idaho. I wonder if some architect will decide to outdo his brethren by creating one that floats with a motor on it so as to provide a moving target.

The continuing development of the sand wedge and its utility for the accomplished player has made use of sand bunkers in areas around greens a problem. The problem is that such bunkers pose virtually no problem for the accomplished player, but provide the mass of more ordinary players with a spectrum of problems ranging from difficult to virtually impossible. Proliferation of such bunkers, therefore, puts the game out of balance. Such development should be countered by increasing the use of grass bunkers in place of sand bunkers in areas around the green. Grass bunkers preserve the skill requirement for the accomplished player while providing a tolerable challenge for the great majority of players.

Architects are being increasingly challenged by the distance the ball is being hit. The tendency to respond to that challenge by designing longer golf courses needs to be resisted. Length as the predominant means of providing a challenge is a cop out. The game and the players do not need it. What they need are courses that will make them think, that will challenge without panicking them, and will leave them with a sense of real accomplishment when they succeed in doing what the architect has challenged them to do. There are numerous examples of what I mean. I will cite but one—the San Francisco Golf Club course. From the white tees it measures 6,350 yards. What it does in those 6,350 yards is provide golfers of all strata of ability with the whole spectrum of thoughtful shot-making.

There also needs to be more thought given to the way each hole looks and to the feelings it evokes when viewed from the tee. There needs to be sensitive concern for the golf aesthetics of the hole and for the fact that the look of the hole sets it up in the player's mind. That look should not only tell him what he has to do; it should stimulate him to do it. A.W. Tillinghast once said that the look of a hole from the tee should provide the player with a stimulating challenge as contrasted with provoking him into a state of hysteria.

Modern equipment for construction and maintenance of courses has not necessarily advanced the cause of effective architecture. In many ways, the advent of the bulldozer has been as perverse an influence on the game as overwatering by misuse of automatic sprinkling systems. These monsters seem to have consumed the imagination to take the terrain as God provided it and find 18 suitable holes in its natural contours and idiosyncrasies. Here again I will cite but one example, and that is the course which, for me at least, is the most consummate combination of the joy, the challenge and the aesthetics that exists anywhere, namely Cypress Point. No one can play that course (which, incidentally, measures only 6,265 yards from the middle tees) without reverence for the genius of Dr. Alister Mackenzie. He used what God gave him. Granted that what God gave him was, as Robert Lewis Stevenson is reported to have said, "The greatest meeting of land and sea upon the face of the planet." The fact remains that he had the wit to use it wisely. Consider what he did:

- He placed three five pars in the first six holes, two of them back-to-back;
- He built two three pars—15 and 16—back-to-back and, in doing so, made two of the most delightfully stimulat-

ing golf holes on the face of the planet.

- He took 600 yards of sand and constructed two par fours (8 and 9) on it so as to provide 600 yards of beautifully exciting, stimulating and satisfying golf.
- He left a clear impression that the design of the course was a joint venture between him and God.

There is so much artistry in effective golf course design that geniuses such as Alister Mackenzie are going to be few and far between. Studying his courses should do a lot to make modern architects more effective.

North Berwick

In a recent trip to the United Kingdom I had the delightful experience of playing North Berwick, which is located on the Firth of Tay about 25 miles east of Edinburgh.

It was a crisp, clear October day in Scotland with an east wind whipping up the whitecaps on the Firth.

Playing that wonderful links course stimulated a host of emotions and thoughts.

North Berwick is a splendid example of how courses were laid out when the architects simply used the terrain with a minimum of changes to its natural features. The result at North Berwick is a combination of wonderfully challenging golf shots with the element of chance, depending on how the ball bounces off the humps and hillocks playing an appropriate role in the game. The player's capacity to use his or her imagination and improvise as necessary gives added dimensions to the experience.

To illustrate the concept of simply adapting the course to the land as it existed, there are two holes at North Berwick that have ancient stone walls as obstacles to be negotiated. One of those holes is a short four-par with the wall running diagonally across the line of the second shot and the green located just over the wall.

As I was enjoying the experience, and in some respects even more the recollections of it, I was moved to think that golfers and golf course architects are taking themselves and the game too seriously.

As the game is now evolving there are two elements that are missing: one is the element of chance, and the other is the related element of whimsy. The existence of those elements in the old courses like North Berwick make the game a lot more fun.

The loss of those elements is primarily due to the pervading focus on the playing of the game by professionals at stroke play for prize money. That form of the game with its emphasis on so-called fairness has developed criteria such as elimination of blind shots, pristine course conditions, including manicured bunkers and consistent, comfortably paced greens on which the ball will come to rest close to where it lands.

That influence has received considerable impetus as an overwhelming portion of new courses are designed by those professional golfers whose concepts about the game have been molded by their very special skills and experience.

While there can be no doubt that precise ball striking should be rewarded, I do not think the rewards should be so predictable as modern courses make them. I also fervently wish that the North Berwicks were not increasingly becoming museum pieces and that designers of new courses would ameliorate their focus on the challenges they are creating with considerably more emphasis on the criteria of how satisfying the playing of their course is going to be.

An Ultimate Contrast

Thanks to a friend with a jet airplane, he and I and two others had a notable experience. In the morning, we played the course in the Nebraska sand hills designed by Ben Crenshaw and Bill Coore, and in the afternoon we played Shadow Creek, the course designed by Tom Fazio on the outskirts of Las Vegas. The contrast between the respective designs of those two courses has to be ultimate.

The Crenshaw/Coore design is laid into those phenomenal sand hills with an absolute minimum of disturbance of the God-given terrain. The experience of playing the course has an ethereal quality. The player has the sense that the terrain had been sculpted by some superior being to accommodate a very special golf course.

The design needed to take account of the winds that sweep across those sand hills. Each of the holes, therefore, could be played with the low, running shot finding the green on the ground.

The course stretches literally for miles into the sand hills where there is no human habitation. This adds an element of adventure in playing it.

Shadow Creek provides the ultimate contrast. Tom Fazio dug a huge hole in the desert, planted 20,000 plus trees, created creeks, waterfalls and ponds and literally manufactured 18 golf holes in a totally man made environment. The imagination that it took (not to mention the money) is awesome. The aesthetics are stunning. The huge hole was dug deep enough so that there is more than an oasis feel to it; there simply is no sense of any desert anywhere in the vicinity.

On this golf course the game is played almost exclusively from point to point in the air. The turf is maintained so that the fairways appear to be made up of green velvet and the green surfaces are billiard table smooth.

The following commentary is not meant as a criticism of a brilliant piece of work by Tom Fazio. It simply is my sense that experiencing the game in a natural setting has an element of communing with nature and an authentic quality that cannot be manufactured.

More Ruminations
and
Reminiscences

Par

There are fundamental concepts in the game of golf that evolved in interesting ways. Take, for example, the concept of par.

While its origins as a golf term and concept are obscure, we can identify reference points in its evolution with some certainty. It is a reasonable guess that the term derived from a stock-market concept relating value of shares of stock to so-called par value.

The first printed reference apparently occurred in a British magazine named "Golf" in 1870. The writer of an article in that publication had asked two British professionals what score would be required to win the British Open at the then 12-hole course at Prestwick. Their response was that perfect play should produce a score of 49. The writer in the piece called this score "par" for Prestwick.

The next reported significant development occurred in 1891 when a gentlemen named Hugh Rotherham organized the first tournament with uniform target scores. That idea quickly spread to other courses.

The concept was advanced by an influential article published in 1898 in England suggesting that par be based on scores that first-class players could be expected to produce.

That concept also took hold and has been the basic scoring premise of the game ever since.

The concept has its proponents and its critics. For example, Bobby Jones wrote that par "is why golf is the greatest of games. You are not playing a human adversary. You are playing a game. You are playing Old Man Par."

Tommy Armour, however, expressed his view as follows:
"It is utterly illogical to expect a person with physical, temperamental and man-

ner of living limitations to be able to play par golf."

In my view, Armour misses the point, which is to have an established standard based on performance expected of a first class player that can be used universally to identify where any player is in the skill pecking order of the game.

The term 'bogey' predated par and originally meant what par means today. Bogey, however, mutated, primarily in America, to finally become fixed as one stroke over par.

History provides no accurate record of how the terms "birdies" and "eagles" become part of the game's language.

While we now take all those terms for granted, it is worth noting that expressing performance with terms such as "bogeys" and "birdies" and "eagles" adds some flavor to communications about the game and that old man Par is an enduring and endearing figure forever challenging us ordinary mortals to achieve the standard he sets for us.

Handicapping

Golf has a whole host of wonderfully distinctive features. One of the more important has to be the concept and system of handicapping.

The term "handicapping" originated in horse racing. Jockeys were handed the odds for a race in a cap in a ceremony that came to be known as hand in cap, from which eventually the term handicap evolved.

It is fitting that the term should have its origins in wagering, because wagering on golf games provided the basic impetus for the development of a system of handicapping.

There were so-called "Bet Books" kept at the golf clubs recording the bets and the results of matches. In an entry made in 1782, reference to handicapping appears in the Bet Book of the Honorable Company of Edinburgh Golfers in the form of the term "half-one," which meant that one player gave the other a stroke at alternate holes.

Eventually English clubs adopted the term handicap. Events with odds or stroke allowances were identified as handicap tournaments.

Various methods of handicapping at individual clubs inevitably led to developing a system which would make the handicaps portable. Such a system, of course, required a governing authority to establish uniform systems of course ratings and handicapping.

It is worth noting that long before the men were able to manage it, the first national system of handicapping was developed around the turn of the century by the English Ladies Golf Union.

It was not until 1911 that the USGA developed the first national USGA handicap system. The problem of rating courses was then solved by rating courses according to the expected score of the national amateur champion.

Systems of handicapping and course rating have been developed that required man and women hours that must accumulate into the millions. These men and women are the unsung heroes and heroines who have made it possible for you and me to have a competitive game of golf regardless of where in this country we are playing and regardless of how much difference there may be in our respective skills.

Those unsung heroes and heroines are responsible for the development of the singular national handicapping system, promulgated by the United States Golf Association and available wherever golf is played in this country.

How distinctive this feature of the game is deserves further emphasis. It provides a universally level playing field for players of all levels of skill so that, for example, you or I can tee it up with Jack Nicklaus playing at the peak of his game. If you or I are playing at the peak of own, our respective handicaps provide us with a reasonable chance of beating him.

We should be humbly grateful for all of the time, thought and devotion that has gone into making such a game available to us.

Golf Television

While the pundits and the politicians pillory television for promulgating sex and violence, they should balance the act with acknowledgment of how useful this medium can be. What it has done for golf certainly is a case in point.

As my involvement on the USGA Executive Committee evolved, the obvious import of television for promoting interest in the game and documenting its history attracted me. That attraction resulted in more than 25 years of personal and professional effort to realize for the USGA mission all that television could do for it.

Money also was a factor in that effort. The revenue from the sale of rights to televise USGA events is a prime element in the USGA's operating budget. That source, therefore, needs to be nurtured for all that it is worth.

Of at least equal import is the production quality of those telecasts. The objectives of identifying the game and its values, attracting and educating players and effectively documenting history as it was being made all are enhanced by quality production.

With regard to both money and quality, it was fortuitous that when I became involved, ABC Sports was the USGA's television resource. Roone Arledge, one of the more creative people in the history of the medium, was then the head of ABC Sports. He dramatically demonstrated how much sports could matter to the medium and conversely how much the medium could matter to sports.

Roone had a special affinity with golf that added to his creativity. His personality made negotiating and working with him a distinctly satisfying experience. Those characteristics attracted remarkably talented people, such as Chuck Howard and Terry Jastrow, to critical roles in the development of

ABC's golf television facility.

That development included innovations which transformed golf television from fixed tower announcer and camera positions on the last four holes to the total coverage that we now enjoy.

Those innovations started with putting reporters on the course with mobile camera units. That put the viewer in the position of the player, and the audience was now enlightened with supplemental commentary on the requirements of the shot the player was facing.

The innovations also included solving all the complex problems required to cover 18 holes. That development was responsive to the desire of the USGA to provide coverage of match play and to give the viewer the total picture of the holes and the shots played in the winning of a U.S. Open.

Those innovations were extended to covering effectively match play so that the United States Amateur Championships could be properly broadcast and documented. This development adds to the disappointment with the decision of the PGA to abandon match play for its championship. As virtually the whole world of professional golf is confined to stroke play, the void left by the change in the PGA Championship becomes increasingly distressing. Since it is a fundamental form of the playing of the game and is the form played in an overwhelming proportion of all the golf played, it is literally a shame that, with relatively minor exceptions, professional tournaments are confined to stroke play.

The evolution of golf on television has been afflicted by how much more effective the video portion has been than the audio. The audio development was affected by the inability of commentators on other sports (e.g. football, baseball and basketball) to adapt to the culture of golf. Those other sports apparently call for virtually constant commentary. Golf, on the other hand, requires commentary confined simply to supplementing the picture so as to provide the viewer with something the viewer otherwise would not understand from the picture. The impulse to talk when silence would be more effective seems to be almost irresistible. It is an anomaly that the commentator generally thought to be the best, Henry Longhurst, was the one who said the least.

It is a matchless medium, nonetheless, for bringing the game to many millions of people around the world and attracting them to add so much to their lives by playing the best of all games.

Inverness

Some interesting history has been made at Inverness.

It was there in 1920 that the great Harry Vardon played in his last U.S. Open Championship. Harry Vardon not only is in the forefront of the pantheon of the game's great players, his swing essentially established the elements of the modern golf swing. His method of gripping the club quickly became the standard. Virtually everyone who plays the game grips the club with what is still identified as "The Vardon Grip."

As the game developed in this country, it adopted the incredible discriminatory social barrier prevalent in the United Kingdom that barred professional golfers from entering the clubhouse. It is an awful commentary on the sociology of the game that this sort of discrimination was prevalent in this country well into this century. My how the sociology has changed! These days amateurs figuratively stand in line to pay thousands of dollars for the privilege of being paired with a professional in a Pro-Am. It was at Inverness where this blight on the game in this country was first exorcised.

Inverness also has the distinction of having had Byron Nelson as its professional. For a number of years Byron presided over the pro shop, gave lessons and developed his game there. During Byron's tenure there was a remarkably talented amateur golfer named Frank Stranahan who was a prominent member. Stranahan, who was the heir to the Champion spark plug fortune, had a significant career that included winning the British Amateur championship and subsequently becoming a successful touring professional. Stranahan apparently thought he was a better player than Byron Nelson and frequently sought to prove it by challenging Byron to play him at Inverness. Byron had no disposition to become competitively involved with a prominent member and managed to avoid the confrontation until one day Stranahan, accompanied by three other very good amateur players, provoked Byron by implying that Byron was afraid to play him. Byron finally agreed to play, but only if he played not just Stranahan, but the best ball of Stranahan and his three friends. Byron then proceeded to settle decisively any question of who was the better player by administering a sound beating to the best ball of the four of them.

It was at Inverness in 1979 that the so-called Hinkle Tree became a chapter in the history of the U.S. Open. In anticipation of that championship some changes were made by George Fazio in the Donald Ross design primarily to accommodate the larger galleries that the Open Championship was attracting. The changes included a new 8th hole that was, and is, an interesting dogleg par five. In the first round, Lon Hinkle discovered a gap in the trees on the left side of the tee through which he played down the 17th fairway, thereby eliminating the dogleg and converting the good par five into a drive and 7-iron hole. That discovery was quickly picked up by the rest of the field. Those of us responsible for the conduct of that Open had a major problem on our hands. Players from separate tees playing to the same fairway and tee shots played from the 8th tee over the heads of people viewing the seventeenth simply were not manageable. We had two choices: move the tee on number 8 forward, which would emasculate a good par five; or plant a tree sufficiently-sized to block the opening to the 17th fairway. We decided on the tree and located and planted it during the night. The next morning I was sitting on the 8th tee when the first pairing arrived and I stayed until the last pairing had hit their tee shots. To put it mildly, the commentary was colorful. The tree, memorialized by the media as the Hinkle Tree, became a front-page story. Notwithstanding a lot of philosophical huffing and puffing, the tree remained, the awful problems were eliminated and the integrity of the 8th hole was preserved.

All of us hooked on golf are indebted to Inverness for all it has contributed to golf history.

The San Francisco City Championship

The special nature of the San Francisco City Golf Championship derives from a number of factors.

It is a championship played at match play, a feature for which all true believers in the game should be cheering.

The stroke play qualifying to determine the 64 players who meet for match play is played on two remarkable golf courses.

I have a love affair with Lincoln Park. I have been blessed with exposure to a wonderful array of golf courses in a large number of countries. I have never seen a course quite like Lincoln. While it is very short, it has a wonderful variety of golf holes providing a stimulating array of challenges. As it winds around the beautiful Palace of the Legion of Honor Museum, it brings you to the 17th tee where you are treated to a stunning view of the Golden Gate and one of the more stimulating par-three holes anywhere.

The effects of a limited maintenance budget, for me at least, provide an added plus to playing Lincoln. It provides a throwback to the way the game was played when grazing sheep maintained the fairways. It may identify me as at least a bit of a nut, but I enjoy the challenges of dealing with a variety of conditions in the course of a round. You certainly have to be able to do that if you are to accomplish a decent round on Lincoln.

The other course, Harding Park, is also special, because the variety and quality of its 18 holes provide a distinctive and stimulating set of challenges. By any standard, it did rank as an outstanding test of golf. (Its condition, however, has been allowed to deteriorate so as to border on being unplayable. I am engaged in a project to see it restored.)

The championship also has a wonderful tradition. Whatever the weather may be and whatever the condition of the golf course, the game is played as it historically was meant to be played—that is, you take the course and the conditions as you find them and make do however you can. As the professional tour has evolved with emphasis on playing the game for money, this feature of the game has been diminished. If the pros are playing on a course with some moisture on it, they frequently will be allowed in the fairway to lift, clean and place the ball within a club length. No such desecration of the true spirit of the game occurs in the San Francisco City Championship. In the 40-plus years I have been playing in the City Championship, there have been a number of occasions when the rainwater was running on the greens so that the putter was useless and the only way to get to the hole was to hit chip shots!

And then there is the field. It is a splendid collection of all sorts of people with a wonderful array of backgrounds and occupations who have come to the game via almost every conceivable access.

It has produced some great champions. In a community about as hooked on golf as a community can get, it is axiomatic that whatever else a player may have done in the game does not mean very much unless he has won The City.

It is only fitting that a world-class city should have a world-class golf championship which has produced world-class champions playing what all True Believers would identify as the true game of golf.

The Ultimate Four-Ball Match

The San Francisco City Golf Championship has produced some great champions. For example, the pantheon of the winners of what is popularly known as "The City" includes Ken Venturi and Harvie Ward.

Those two champions achieved a host of distinctions in the course of their respective careers. Among the more impressive of those distinctions is one that they shared that received no publicity and was witnessed by only a handful of spectators.

It was a four-ball match in which they were partners and which has to be the most brilliantly played four-ball match ever played anywhere.

The match was played at the Cypress Point Club on a weekday afternoon in 1956. They were matched against Ben Hogan and Byron Nelson.

The first hole was halved in par. The second was halved in birdies, the third was halved in birdies, the fourth was halved in birdies, the fifth was halved in birdies, the sixth was halved in birdies, the seventh was halved in birdies, the eighth was halved in birdies and the ninth was halved in birdies. The team of Ben Hogan and Byron Nelson, therefore, reached the turn 8-under-par so that they managed to be all even with the two San Francisco City amateur champions!

On the 10th hole Hogan holed a wedge shot for an eagle to win the hole by a stroke. The two teams then proceeded to halve 11 with birdies, 12 with birdies, 13 with birdies, 14 with pars, 15 with birdies, the glorious 16th with birdies and the 17th with birdies. When they reached 18, therefore, 14 holes had been halved with birdies, two holes had been halved with pars and Hogan's eagle on 10 was the difference that put Hogan and Nelson one up.

Ken Venturi holed a long putt to birdie 18, leaving Hogan with a 15 footer for a birdie to preserve the one up margin. Hogan calmly put the ball in the center of the cup!

Hogan and Nelson therefore had a best ball of 17 under par. They needed every bit of it to achieve a sensational victory over the two amateurs by the narrowest of margins.

Hogan produced a 63 that afternoon. The four players, in the aggregate, were 27 under par, so their average score was $1/4$ stroke over 65 on a very demanding golf course!

In a recent interview, Byron Nelson said this about the match: "All four of us played about as well as we could play."

That strikes me as a bit of an understatement.

Maximizing
the Benefits

We can, of course, learn a lot from the great players about the mechanics of hitting a golf ball. There is much more, however, that we can learn from them that is even more important because it relates to maximizing the satisfaction we can get from a round of golf.

First, there is the thought expressed by Bobby Jones to the effect that golf is a game of inches; that is, the 5½ between our ears.

That thought leads to the Ben Hogan credo, which was to approach every shot with the perception that the playing of it is a privilege that involves a commensurate responsibility to devote to the playing of each shot all of the resources we can muster.

Related to that is the example of Byron Nelson, constricted by his age and a bad hip to hitting the ball relatively puny distances with his hands, managing to get a full measure of pleasure simply out of doing the best that he could.

And then there is the philosophy exemplified by the approach that Walter Hagen took in playing the game; that is, while you are giving it your all and making do with whatever skill you may have, you should not forget to smell the flowers along the way.

The Hagen philosophy deserves some emphasis. With the possible exception of skiing, golf has the most beautiful playing fields of any sport. In the throes of dealing with the difficulties and disappointments with which most of us mortals have to deal in the course of a round of golf, we can literally lose sight of the aesthetics of the setting in which we are struggling. When we do so, we are depriving ourselves of one of the prime benefits of being hooked on golf.

The most effective expression I have ever heard or read about how we should think about the playing of the game is in Michael Murphy's masterful book titled, *Golf in the Kingdom*. For those who have read *Golf in the Kingdom*, it is worth rereading. For those who have not read it, until you read that book, you cannot claim to have considered all of the dimensions that approaching the game with the right mental attitude can add to the experience of playing it.

There is a message here more important than any golf score we might achieve: there is a kingdom attainable on every golf course in every round of golf, a kingdom that each of us can create for ourselves if we pursue the grail that is the game in the right frame of mind.

Dealing with Failure

A friend of mine was suffering grievously from the effects of a series of bad rounds of golf. I was moved to write him the following letter.

Dear Jan:

As I listened to your lament on about how a lousy round of golf had afflicted not just your emotions but your very being, I had a number of reactions. They included empathy, sympathy, compassion and the disposition to provide advice which herewith I presume to provide.

There are few important involvements in life that can elicit so much advice from so many advisors as a poor soul struggling with his or her golf game. It behooves the advisee, therefore, to be discriminating about the advisor to whom to listen.

I, therefore, proffer my credentials.

I have been pursuing the grail that is the game for more than 70 years with a fervor of intensity even you would find difficult to imagine. In the course of those 70 plus years I have played at least 4,000 rounds of golf. I can classify those rounds (with some room for overlap) as follows:

- rounds in which I played encouragingly near my potential: 10%;
- rounds in which I played tolerably near my potential: 20%;
- rounds that were abject disasters (e.g., in The Pacific Coast Amateur at Pebble Beach many years ago when I was in the hunt in the third round and over a stretch of six holes in the middle of the round failed to get the ball airborne!): 10%;
- in 50% of the rounds played in particular settings that gave them special significance, my performance has ranged from abysmal to intolerable (e.g., of all the rounds I have been privileged to play with Tom

Watson, in only a couple have I played tolerably);
- the rounds that have evolved as I hoped they would and realistically thought they should: 35%.

There are a number of other premises, both statistical and substantive, for qualifying me as an advisor to the golflorn, but the foregoing should suffice.

Given the pervading lamentable experiences I have suffered with the game, how have I managed not just to retain, but continue to build on, my abiding love and enthusiasm for the playing of it?

- first and foremost, in the inevitable debriefing of the round I have played, I never dwell on the bad shots; I only think about them in terms of identifying the causes and resolving to rectify them;
- conversely, I focus on the good shots recalling the satisfactions I experienced in the playing of them and citing them to myself as evidence that I realistically can play the game effectively. (I am reminded of a friend who wearily sat down in a locker round after an awful round and said, "Damn it all! If I could just get rid of those one or two good shots I hit in the course of a round I could give up this lousy game!");
- when I play a round in which I did not hit one shot worth recalling, I simply exorcise the round from my experience so that it is as if I have never played it;
- finally, I remain absolutely convinced that the breakthrough to consistently good golf is about to occur. The efficacy of that conviction includes:
  - that it could occur on the very next swing;
  - that it adds to the anticipation of the next round;
  - that the expectation includes the realization that when it occurs, it will render all the lousy shots I have hit and lousy rounds I have played utterly meaningless.

And so I say to you, Jan, do not indulge in self-flagellation or, even worse, self pity, be of good heart and spirit and develop the conviction that the sword will come out of the rock—all you have to do is to manage to grip it properly!

The Yips

I dislike afflicting the atmosphere with a horror story, but any chronicle of my golf experience must include it. Furthermore the horror in the story is an episode of the yips and no chronicle of the game could be complete without reference to that sometimes fatal disease.

No one who has not suffered this awful affliction can begin to understand how awful it is. Regrettably I am all too qualified to address the subject because I am a recovering yipper.

There may possibly be some reader whose golf life has been so insulated and isolated that he or she does not know what is meant by the verb to yip. What it means is be so overwhelmed by grotesque fear of missing a short putt as to lose control of the putter. That loss of control can take two basic forms: inability to move the putter at all, which was the affliction Ben Hogan suffered at the end of his career; or the putter, as if in the hands of demons, wildly stabs at the ball.

The yips from which I am recovering took the latter form. My horror story is to have experienced the mother of all yips.

I was playing in the Crosby. Tom Watson was my partner. We were paired with Greg Norman and Kerry Packer. We were playing Pebble Beach on a beautiful Saturday. As we played the 18th hole, Watson was in the hunt for the pro title and our team was on the border line of making the cut in the Pro-Am. I was convinced that we needed a birdie on that hole to make it. When I managed to get 20 feet from the hole in three on that glorious par five with a stroke on the hole and Watson whistled a wedge to four feet from the cup, I thought we had it made. I carefully maneuvered my first putt about 14 inches below the hole. As I watched Watson work on his four-footer, I was jolted by the realization that I was praying he would make it. He missed. As I stood over my 14-incher, my mind went completely blank. I have no recollection of moving the putter, but I do know that the putter struck the ball twice and that the ball ended up 5 feet past the hole!

In addition to Watson, Norman and Packer, that humiliation was witnessed by my entire large family, a lot of my friends and literally thousands of other people filling the stands around the 18th green.

I do not know how I managed to deal with the end of round protocol or with my family and friends or how I managed to get back to the house where we were staying. A stiff drink helped the recovery along so that I could start dealing with how I could manage the rest of my life. I got a faint ray of hope from the thought that I might be able to continue to play golf, provided, of course, that I only played by myself. It was painfully clear, however, that I neither could nor would ever again play a competitive round of golf.

Having reached that traumatic conclusion, I called tournament headquarters to learn what time Watson would be playing on Sunday. When the lady on the line gave me the time, I asked with whom he was playing, and she replied, "with Sandy Tatum, Sandy Lyle and Chuck Van Linge." So we had made the cut after all!

No one in golf's kingdom can ever have been happier than I was to be on that first tee at Pebble Beach on that Sunday playing in the final round of the Crosby with Tom Watson. I became at that moment a recovering yipper and I am an example of the message of hope that there is not just life, but much more important, there is golf, after the yips.

Epilogue

Epilogue

The love affair brokered by my father has lasted for more than seventy years. Furthermore, as the skills, such as they were, diminish, the affair gets more rather than less intense. These reminiscences and ruminations provide some indication of how profound has been the impact of that love affair on my life. It is comforting to think that somewhere along the way I may have made a small downpayment on the monumental debt that I owe to it.